D1584223

My Family, My Friends, My Life

These Lifted Me Up Along the Way

Isabell von der Waldesruh

outskirts
press

My Family, my Friends, my Life

I was born on a Monday, January 3, 1944, in the picturesque city of Heppenheim an der Bergstrasse, Hesse, Germany. Half-timbered houses and vineyards characterize this medieval town. The ruins of the castle Starkenburg that was built 1065/66 A.D. attracts many visitors. Its climate is the warmest in the area. Many famous people have visited this town, among them the 56th Secretary of State, Henry Kissinger, on September 22, 1973, and Martin Buber, an Austrian-born Israeli Jewish philosopher who lived there from 1916 – 1938 along with many other prominent people.

While my mother was in labor, her cousin's wife, Hedwig Helfrich, arrived, also being in labor. My mother called out, "You, too, Hedwig?" Then they hugged each other. Aunt Hedwig's daughter, Hedi, arrived in this world just three hours after me. During our school years, Hedi spent summers at our house in Kirschhausen, a suburb of Heppenheim. Hedi lived with her parents and her brother in Weinheim an der Bergstrasse.

During the Middle Ages, Kirschhausen belonged with the five other villages Erbach, Unter- and Ober-Hambach, Sonderbach, and Wald-Erlenbach to *Villa Heppenheim*. The inhabitants of these six villages were one unit with St. Peter Basilica. This all dates back to January 20, 773, in connection with Charlemagne the Great. On January 1st, 1972, these six villages had become each a district of Heppenheim. Their names remained the same.

I am somewhat curious about my zodiac sign, but do not live by it. *Capricorn* or "The Goat" December 23 – January 20

Capricorns are stable, serious, and practical. They are reliable and capable of incredible perseverance. They are resourceful, honest, and set high standards for themselves.

Capricorns are careful planners who can achieve great results because of their exceptional organizing ability.

Capricorns value tradition. While demanding, they are fair. The ruling planet is Saturn. Stone is Garnet. It is one of the most diverse gemstones in nature, found in Africa, Australia, India, Russia, South America, and the United States in Arizona and Idaho. Garnet comes in many different colors and shades. Ruby red is the most common color for Capricorn.

Capricorn's lucky number is four and lucky day is Saturday.

My family is Roman Catholic and three days after my birth, on the Feast of the Epiphany of Our Lord, I was baptized with the name Rita Lulay at St. Peter's Basilica in Heppenheim. My Godmother was my father's sister, Anna Luise Lulay.

Interesting facts about my surname Lulay – Psalm 27:

I have the faith that I surely will see
God's goodness throughout my life
Hope in God and have courage
Trust in God all day long
Hope in God and have courage
Trust that your heart will be strong.

This part starts in Hebrew with Lulay.

I claim this as my own.

World War II was in full swing when I was born. Children born in 1944 were called the children of the "Stunde Null" or "Zero Hour". It refers to May 8, 1945 at midnight, the end of World War II. Germany's cities lay in ruins. Many families had lost everything. There was nothing available for newborns or infants under normal conditions at the beginning of their lives were able to get. Even today, many who did survive this tragedy say "How did we manage this? How did we combat hunger? Where did we go to feel warm and protected? From where did we get diapers?" Many had to start anew and made out of old items new ones. Toys were made out of beat-up cans, wood, and metal pieces. However, the "Zero Hour" was not the same for everybody. We lived in the country side and did not experience the destruction of cities like Dresden, Hamburg, Berlin, Bremen, and other big cities. During air raids, military chaff, my older sisters called it tinsel, appeared in the sky, to hide aircrafts from radar detection. During the month of January, 1944, the following events occurred:

01/04 The 1st Ukrainian Front of the Red Army enters Poland.

01/12 The Italian Foreign Minister and Mussolini's son-in-law were executed by Mussolini's revived Fascist government sympathizers

01/17 The first battle of Monte Cassino begins

01/19 Red Army troops push westward toward the Baltic countries.

01/20 The Royal Air Force drops 2,300 tons of bombs on Berlin.

01/22 Allies begin operation Shingle.

01/23 The British destroyer HMS Janus is sunk off Anzio.

01/24 The Allied Forces have a major setback on the Gari River.

01/24 In German-occupied Belgium, the Social Pact, detailing plans for post-war social reform, is secretly signed.

01/28 The Russian Army completes encirclement of two German Army corps at the Korsun pocket, south of Kiev. Two-thirds of the Germans escape in the breakout next month with the loss of most heavy equipment.

01/30 United States troops invade Majuro, Marshall Islands. Japanese kill 44 suspected spies in the Homfreyganj massacre.

01/31 American forces land on Kwajalein Atoll and other islands.

1944 D-Day
1945 WWII ends

My father, tall and slender, black-haired, loved to puff on a pipe, was stationed in Stalingrad, Russia, now called Volgograd, where the bloodiest battle of World War II was fought. Many lost their lives because of hunger, froze to death, or just didn't survive the cruel onslaught of the Russian Army. My father's rank was a Sergeant in the German Army. He was wounded three times, January 14, 1943, January 21, 1944, and July 17, 1944. One injury was from a gunshot wound to his upper right arm, which never really healed. Nevertheless, he refused to get his arm amputated, despite the infections that he had to endure from time to time. He received the Purple Heart in silver, which I have in my possession among some other medals and his compass. The temperatures in Stalingrad during winter dropped to 40 degrees below zero.

None of those who fought on the eastern front was aware of what was going on with Hitler, the so-called Fuehrer, and his diabolical works.

I can trace back to the 16th century my ancestors on my father's side. I was not so lucky to go back that far with my mother's ancestors. Daddy loved theatre and all kinds of humor while my mother enjoyed music.

ISABELL VON DER WALDESRUH

She knew almost every song under the sun from beginning to end. We sang a lot as a family and my oldest sister, Marianne, inherited my father's acting talent. She always had major roles to play. When she memorized and practiced at home, I mastered many things along with her. The song about Mutter Polke is still strong in my mind. I don't think that I was ten years old at that time.

Ich bin die Mutter Polke	I'm the Mother Polke
Verheiratet schon lang	Got married long time ago
Hab' als Frau aus dem Volke	Own as a woman from this nation
Ein feines Moebelmang	Much fine furniture
Ein Schrank, ne Bank, Tisch,	A cabinet, a bench, table,
Stuhl und Bett ganz schlicht	Chair, and bed, all very simple
Jawohl die Mutter Polke	Yes, the Mother Polke
Ist gesetzlich eingericht	Is all set up as required by law
Einst war ich ganz versessen	Once, I was very obsessed
Auf meinen Anton doch	About my Anton
Und haette bald gefressen	And almost ate him up
Vor lauter Lieb' ihn noch	Out of love
Doch heut, ihr Leut,	But today, dear people,
seh an ich den Kumpan	When I look at this pal

| da aergere ich mich immer | I get so angry about myself |
| dass ich's damals nicht getan | That I didn't do it at that time |

My parents, Hans and Maria Lulay, got married right after Christmas on Monday, December 26, 1932. They had three girls before I was born. Maria Barbara, called Marianne, was ten, Irene Katharina eight, and Agnes Katharina was five years old. It was understood that I was the long awaited little boy and Joachim was the name chosen for me. When I had arrived, my mother was then desperate for a girl's name. She asked the midwife whether she knew a great girl's name. Frau Helfert replied, "Rita is a nice name." My mother responded, "Yes, she will be named Rita." When my mother had returned home from the hospital, she wrote to my father, "Rita was born on January 3rd and is healthy." Later on, when Frau Helfert had a daughter of her own, she named her Rita, too.

March 27, 1945, was a mild spring day. Around 4:00 p.m. in the afternoon, American solders walked up Heppenheimerstrasse (main street). There were also six Germans with machine guns. The Germans and the advancing American infantrymen got into a battle. An American officer got killed. In order to protect the village, the carpenter Joest and the local priest Pfarrer

Weber of Kirschhausen informed the Americans that the person who fired the shots and killed one of the Americans was not a local. Pfarrer Weber had always warned about the Nazi. On Wednesday, March 28, tanks rolled through the streets for hours. Uncle Gregor, who was back home from the war and wore civilian clothes, was called to a neighbor's house in Kirschhausen to help deliver a cow. Upon his arrival, Americans noticed on his shoes that he was a member of the Wehrmacht and arrested him. Grandmother Barbara employed a French prisoner-of-war who recognized the impending threat and went straight over and stood in front of Uncle Gregor. An officer, who had joined at a later time, prevented the worst. Grandmother Barbara begged with tears streaming down her cheeks to do no harm to her son. She didn't speak any English. Despite her anguish, they transferred Uncle Gregor to a prison in Worms. There he was interrogated by the security. "Without two witnesses for the persecution we condemn no one," said the interrogator. They searched the party headquarters of the NSDAP (Nazi Party) in Frankfurt and there were no damaging moments registered. After five weeks, Uncle Gregor was allowed to go home.

The war ended on September 2, 1945. When the Red Army reached downtown in the battle for Berlin, Adolf Hitler committed suicide in the afternoon on April 30,

1945. Germany had lost the war. My father had escaped to avoid becoming a prisoner of war. He got rid of his uniform. He had met kind people who donated civilian clothes to him. He was then able to travel home unnoticed. My mother always shared with us children his amazing homecoming.

My sisters and my mother stood in front of our house on Heppenheimerstrasse 31 in Kirschhausen, a suburb of Heppenheim at that time, chatting with the neighbors from across the street. It was a pleasant Sunday evening in October of 1944. We had arrived home from a prayer service at church. I was told that Marianne had called out, "Down the street, at the mill of the Mitsch Family, walks Papa." Mama, holding me in her arms, said to her, "That can't be, Marianne!" The longer my mother stared at this man in civilian clothes, the more she recognized my Dad's gait, but he was a walking skeleton. It must have been an unbelievable shock and joy at the same time for my mother to see Daddy coming home alive. She was so deeply connected to him that she sensed when he was in grave danger, lying somewhere in a ditch so far away in an extremely hostile land. She experienced many of these premonitions during the middle of lonely and scary nights. Her faith carried her through much darkness and anxiety during this time. I was ten months old when I met my father for the first time.

It seemed that it took a while for me to get used to this stranger in our house. Whenever I was asked where Papa was, I pointed at his picture which stood in the antique oak cabinet in our living-room. Later, on several occasions, I envisioned myself, either in a dream or awake, lying in my crib in a white romper experiencing an air raid alarm.

My mother and my sisters always told me that I was a good baby. I rarely cried, smiled a lot, sucked always on my two middle fingers, and had beautiful chubby cheeks. I do recognize those in my baby pictures.

My mother is holding me when I was an infant.

The house we had rented while my father was gone had a fenced-in garden, where my mother planted lettuce, carrots, and other vegetables for us to eat because food was rationed. The owner of the house, Herr Ulrich, lived upstairs. We were lucky that we lived in the country because food was more readily available through self-help like gardening. The people who lived in the city received CARE packages. These were by far not enough to live on. Our house had a built-in hen house with tiny windows. My mother, no newcomer to farm work, raised chickens. We had always fresh eggs and once in a while a chicken to eat.

1946 Nuremberg Trial
        "Iron Curtain" speech
1947 Dead Sea Scrolls discovered

Our Grandmother Barbara with my three aunts lived in the same village. They cared for the large farm and they were generous to us, too, by giving us potatoes, milk, butter, and fruit. In return, my mother, Marianne, Irene, and Agnes worked in the fields, even after Daddy had returned home from the war. The cousins closer to my age joined in the fun we had playing with Dolly, our grandmother's small white and black, long-haired dog. Aunt Margret, my father's older sister, or Grandmother Barbara usually remained at the house, took care of the household and cooked dinner. They had more than one spinning wheel. Grandmother Barbara worked so fast, and it was always fun to watch how she managed to turn the yarn. They also had a male servant who fed the horses and cows and cleaned their stalls. When Aunt Margret or Grandmother Barbara sent Dolly outside to deliver a message to us in the fields, she wrote it on a piece of paper, placed it in Dolly's muzzle, and instructed the dog where to go. Dolly arrived safely with the given message. One day, while we were out in the fields, Dolly started barking. When everyone rushed over to the spot where he was barking at, we saw a turtle about the size of a dinner plate. Nobody had any idea where it came from. We named the turtle, Gretel. She was taken to my Grandmother Barbara's garden, where she lived for many more years. Gretel was blind in one eye and loved to eat plums. In the wintertime, she stayed in the cellar.

Whenever we worked or played out in the field, we enjoyed eating Grandmother Barbara's home baked rye bread with a crunchy crust, topped with homemade butter and plum puree. This memory is still fresh in my mind and in my taste buds like it happened yesterday. The following song is still strong in my mind because it reflects what needed to be done in the fall and the closeness and cheerfulness we felt with Mother Earth when we were singing.

Gold'ne Aehre, du musst   Golden ear, you must fall
fallen

Gold'ne Aehre, du must fallen	Golden ear, you must fall
Aehre reif am Halm	Ear, heavy on the stalk
Darfst nicht mehr in Wogen wallen	You are no longer able to move in waves
Sinkst von meinem Arm	You sink from my arm
Dass sich Fleiss und Arbeit naehre	That diligence and work pay off
Reif im Sonnenstrahl	And mature in sunbeam
Falle, falle, Gold'ne Aehre	Fall, fall, golden ear
Alles faellt einmal, faellt einmal	Everything will fall one day fall one day
Faellt einmal, faellt einmal	Fall one day, fall one day

Abends bindet man die Garben	In the evening we bind the sheaves
Fuehrt sie froehlich heim	And bring them gladly home
Menschen kamen auch und starben	Even men came and died
Alles kehret heim	Everything will return home
Einst auch geh' ich Schnittermaedchen	One day, I, the reaper girl, will go
So dahin, dahin	the same way, same way
Und es dreht sich auch kein Blaettchen	Not even a leaf will care about me

| Dass ich nicht mehr bin, nicht mehr bin | That I'm no longer around no longer around |
| Nicht mehr bin, nicht mehr bin | No longer around, no longer around |

Einst auf meinem Grabeshuegel	One day, on my grave on the hill
Wachsen Bluemchen auf	Will grow little flowers
Und ein Geist mit goldnem Fluegel	And a spirit with a golden wing
Schwingt sich himmelauf	Soars heavenwards
Fremde kommen dann und pfluecken	Strangers will come and pick
Diese Blumen ab	These flowers
Streuen dann mit nassen Blicken	And sprinkle with wet eyes
Rosen auf mein Grab, auf mein Grab	Roses on my grave, on my grave
Auf mein Grab, auf mein Grab	On my grave, on my grave

Grandmother Barbara had a half-brother who lived in Erbach, about a half-an-hour walk from Kirschhausen. We all called him Uncle Hannes, which stands for Johannes, Hans, and Johann. He visited every Sunday and loved our grandmother dearly. Grandmother Barbara had another half-brother. He emigrated from

Germany to Columbus, Ohio, when he was very young. He never got married or had any children. When Grandmother Barbara had passed away, the entire Lulay Family received some of the inheritance from my Grandmother Barbara's half-brother estate. My cousin, Gerda McCormick, who lives in Austin, Texas, and was married to a G.I., approached the JAG. They assisted in this process and our inheritance was cleared.

For several months, Marianne and Irene had no school during the war. Rats with long tails ran occasionally around in our attic. At times, they even came into the upstairs bedrooms, where Marianne and Irene slept. On several occasions, they came running and screaming downstairs because they heard a rat. When Agnes and Irene had scarlet fever and were quite ill with very high fever, Mama kept both of them on the lower level until they got over this serious illness. They didn't have to worry about rats coming near their beds. Most of these stories I learned from my mother and my sisters. However, I do have distant memories of that house with its long, narrow kitchen. At the end of the kitchen was a window. Because the kitchen was so restricted, there was a narrow table along the wall. I remember vaguely about the hen house and the day to day living there. The rest of the house is very obscure in my memory.

ISABELL VON DER WALDESRUH

With my father now back home and the war over, the next step my parents contemplated and discussed was to build their own home. Germany lay in ruins, but most of the countryside was intact. They dreamt of a house they would call their own. My Dad was the oldest son of his parents. His father, my grandfather, had passed away from blood poisoning while he delivered a dead calf, and he had an open cut in his hand. Antibiotics or penicillin had not been discovered yet. He knew Latin and when he heard the doctor say, "*ipse morietur,*" he understood that he must die. So he passed away December 7, 1917, when my father was ten years old.

In those days, the oldest son always inherited the homestead. With this in mind, my father had studied agriculture before the war. However, with his severely damaged right arm as a result from the gunshot wound, he was not able to take over the farm. Grandmother Barbara offered my father a building plot as a substitute, which was located at the Honerbachstrasse in Kirschhausen. Adjacent to the plot was an acre of land. On the right side of that piece of land grew fir and oak trees and hedges of sloe and elderberries. On the left, there was a creek flowing through Kirschhausen. My Dad's cousin lived on the other side of the creek and was a beekeeper. This was the perfect place to build our new home. However, it was easier said than done. After the war there was no material available to construct a house, nor any currency to purchase parts or even nails. In Kirschhausen, everybody knew each other and would lend a hand to those in need. Clay was in abundance at our property.

1948   Berlin Airlift
         Gandhi assassinated
         Israel founded

Soon, Papa got a job at the company Carl Freudenberg in Weinheim, a diversified group of companies that was founded in 1849. Money became a little more fluid, but it was still not enough. Our family of six had to be fed and clothed from one income. We needed to start from whatever was available to build the house. My mother's brothers, my dad's cousin, and many friends got together and offered to help. Even my mother worked all day long on the construction site, stirring cement and other types of work that only men are accustomed to doing. Marianne's job was to look after me, take care of me during the day and later on after Kindergarten, prepare dinner for me, and bring me to bed in the evening. My father was also the commander of the fire department from 1937 – 1939 and again from 1948 until 1951.

Grandmother Barbara had four sons. Three returned home after the war. In 1947, out of thanksgiving, she ordered a granite Marian wayside shrine to be erected. Later on, in the 1970s when I lived in Jonesboro, Georgia, and attended ceramic classes, my sister Marianne informed me that someone had vandalized that shrine and damaged the Madonna severely. I painted one and sent it to my sister. To this day, this Madonna has a permanent place in my grandmother's shrine overseeing Kirschhausen where I grew up.

Playing in the fields or gleaning ears of grain was fun. My cousin, Horst, he was three years older than me and had always the craziest ideas, was well known for biting off the head of crickets. Alone the thought of it makes me shiver or throw up. His sister, Gerda, who was ten months older than I am, played a trick on me once. Later on, when we were already in elementary school, she asked me after school whether I would like to go home with her for a little while. Since she lived on the way leading to my house, I agreed. They had three, big, white geese roaming around in their courtyard, and when the geese spotted me, they raced toward me, stretching their long necks even higher and their orange beaks opened and closed quacking. I was afraid that they would bite me. The way they acted was almost worse than dogs. Their vocalization was quite vicious. Gerda chased them away, but one was still trying to catch my skirt. Gerda managed to control its fury. I then went with her to the cellar where she offered me the most beautiful golden-yellow pear. This pear was so tempting that I bit into it without washing it. As soon as I had acquired some taste, a piece almost got stuck in my throat, but I was able to spit it out. I yelled at Gerda, "Do you want to poison me?" She just couldn't stop laughing and then told me that it was a quince. I learned from this experience, even though I was still young, not to have blind trust. Always weigh things out.

Sisters of Divine Providence fled to Kirschhausen during the war to avoid Hitler's persecution. Some of them were cloistered and Sister Eleonore became the Kindergarten teacher. Mama enrolled me in Kindergarten, which included preschool. She knew that I would be in good hands with Sister Eleonore. I learned how to make stars out of ironed straws, which were then used on our Christmas tree. In Christmas plays, Sister Eleonore always assigned the role of an angel to me. Sometimes I wondered, why can't I be a shepherd or Mary, but Sister knew best. The Christmas trees had sparkling stars made out of aluminum foil. We worked on the stars during Advent, the season before Christmas. Who could make the best and most sparkling star the children always competed with one another. The air was filled with anticipation of what was about to happen. Mama always told me you have red cheeks like freshly baked apples because I always felt very hot before a play, especially when I had a speaking part. After the play, we shared butter cookies and milk which the parents provided.

Throughout the year, the children took naps on straw cots in the afternoon. They were not particularly comfortable. Each child received a tiny pillow and a blanket. They belonged to the school. Most of the time, I found it extremely boring to lie down and do nothing. However, Sister Eleonore had all of us under control. I liked her a lot. Working on handicrafts was my favorite occupation. Pasting and organizing pictures was a lot of fun, too. We did some drawing as well. During the morning hours, Sister Eleonore kept us busy with counting, learning the alphabet, and simple math. Some children would have preferred to go outdoors all the time, but I enjoyed learning and doing things with my hands. Playing games on rainy days while sitting in a circle was a lot of fun, too. I learned a song about a frog and then I had to sing it all the time whoever wanted to hear me sing.

| Es ging ein Frosch spazieren | A frog went for a walk |
| An einem Sonntagnachmittag | On a Sunday afternoon |

Und wollte sich frisieren	And wanted to style its hair
An einem gruenen Gartenhaag	On a green garden hague
Da kam der Herr Frisierer	Along came Mister Barber
Und sprach, Ihr Froesche seid ein Chor	And said, you frogs you are a chorus
Ich kann Euch nicht frisieren	I cannot style you
Ihr habt ja gar kein Haar	You do not have any hair

Kindergarten picture with Fraeulein Reinholdt

At 5:00 p.m., my sister Marianne picked me up from Kindergarten. We walked to our house that was being built. I hugged and chatted with Mama and Papa and all the other workers. It was always for a brief time only. I remember Herr Martin with his white hair. He was a bricklayer and always had to leave at 5:00 p.m. when I arrived from Kindergarten. He lived in Fischweiher, which belonged to Heppenheim, and he had a good 30 minutes to walk home. Nobody owned a car at that time in 1947/1948. Marianne enjoyed the responsibility to bring me home and take care of me. Since I had my main meal in Kindergarten, she prepared just a light supper for me. Then I had to go to bed. I hated that.

There was a slope on the west side of our property at the Honerbachstrasse. In order to protect the house from mud sliding down the hill when it rained, my parents and the other workers built a wall in front of it, which later became a shed. While they were placing the rock on top of the other and adding cement, Uncle Franz had the idea to get a glass bottle and a piece of paper and everyone present had to sign this paper with the date, myself included. Even though I was not in elementary school yet, I was able to write my name. Then the paper was placed into the glass bottle, sealed, and walled in.

One afternoon, I was standing at the Honerbachstrasse when Sister Eleonore walked by in her habit. She looked at my arm and said, "You have a mirror on your arm." I looked at my arms because I didn't quite understand what she actually meant. I looked at both arms and then discovered on my right arm what Sister Eleonore called a mirror. I felt ashamed and stared at the ground. Earlier I had a runny nose and instead of using a handkerchief to wipe my nose clean, I used the sleeve of my arm.

Sunday was the only day I was able to spend time with Mama and Papa. In the morning, we attended Mass, and in the afternoon, we walked over to the Honerbachstrasse to our house to be. The conversation at the dinner table was mainly about the house and what was the next step.

On Friday, June 18, 1948, there was a national radio announcement in Germany: "The military powers of Great Britain, France, and the United States have passed the first law for the reform of the German monetary system. It will become valid as of June 20th. The old German currency will become invalid following the change. The new currency will be called the 'Deutsche Mark'." The Germans had lost confidence in their previous currencies, the Reichsmark, the Rentenmark, and the allied military mark. There was enough money floating around, but they couldn't buy anything with it.

Russia was not happy with this development and The Berlin Blockade (24 June 1948 – 12 May 1949) was one of the first major international crises of the Cold War. During the multinational occupation of post-World War II Germany, the Soviet Union blocked the Western Allies' railway, road, and canal access to the sectors of Berlin under Western control. The Soviets offered to drop the blockade if the Western Allies withdrew the Deutsche Mark from West Berlin.

However the Western Allies responded by organizing the Berlin airlift (26 June 1948 – 30 September 1949) to carry supplies to the people of West Berlin, a difficult undertaking given the city's population.

By the spring of 1949, the airlift was in full swing and quite successful, and by April it was delivering more cargo than had previously been transported into the city by rail. On 12 May 1949, the USSR lifted the blockade of West Berlin. The Berlin Blockade revealed the ideological and economic differences for postwar Europe.

Shortly before our move into the house, it was already winter but had not snowed yet, Aunt Gretel with Marga, Uncle Hans with Aunt Maria, and Aunt Katie who had arrived a few days earlier from Port Shepstone, South Africa, took a trip to Kirschhausen and inspected our almost finished house. Aunt Katie visited her mother in Ober-Abtsteinach and the rest of the family. Aunt Katie emigrated from Germany to South Africa when she was 18 years old, married a Frenchman, and later on had four children. When the situation in Germany improved, Mama used to send German presents to South Africa, and Aunt Katie sent us toys which were not available in Germany. I remember when we received two little dogs with magnets on the bottom along with some other items. We played with these toys for hours and stored them in a special drawer in the kitchen that we wouldn't lose them.

Finally the day had arrived to move into our new home. It was Thursday, December 23, 1948, and close to Christmas. My major concern was how will I move my belongings, and doll with carriage, to the new home. It was only a five-minute walk. I was overjoyed when I finally arrived at the house with everything intact. On Christmas Eve, our parents had no presents for us because they had no money to purchase anything, and there was nothing to buy to begin with. At the last minute, Mama took the bus to Heppenheim and went to the Straub store and found for me a porcelain head of a baby doll. The eyes opened and closed. The right cheek had a crack. Arms, legs, and body were made out of clothes and stuffed with pieces of cloth. The face was baby-like and real looking. My sisters became coloring pencils. The times were difficult for my parents, but we children were happy, and our parents were proud of us.

It was a big change to move to a new place, but we spent Christmas in our new house. I don't have much recollection of that first Christmas, but Mama always said that I liked that doll so much. When I held it in my arms for the first time and saw the eyes open and close, I called out, "She can sleep!" This was so important to me. The doll is still fresh in my memory. On the neck of the porcelain head was some writing imprinted which could have read MADE IN GERMANY. Agnes and I tried to decipher it but it was impossible. We figured out that her name must be AMGYMUNG. We had a real Christmas tree with real candles, beautifully decorated balls, tinsel, and a very pointed top. My mother decorated the tree on Christmas Eve as every year and nobody was allowed to go into that room afterwards until it was official. One of our favorite songs was:

Der Christbaum ist der schoenste Baum	The Christmas tree is the most beautiful tree
Den wir auf Erden kennen	We know on earth
Ein Garten klein im engen Raum	A small garden in a tiny room
Wie lieblich blueht der Wunderbaum	How lovely blooms this miracle tree
Wenn seine Lichter brennen, ja brennen	When its lights shine, yes, shine

Denn sieh' in jener
Wundernacht
Ist einst der Herr geboren
Der Heiland, der uns se-
lig macht
Haett er den Himmel
nicht gebracht
Waer alle Welt verloren,
verloren…

See, during this miracu-
lous night
Was once born our Lord
The Savior who will
bless us
If he had not made
heaven
All the world would be
lost…

Drum lass ihn ein, es ist
kein Traum
Er waehlt Dein Herz zum
Garten
Will pflanzen in den en-
gen Raum
Den allerschoensten
Wunderbaum
Will Deiner treulich war-
ten,….ja warten

Let him in, it is no
dream
He chooses your heart
for his garden
He will plant in this
small room
The most beautiful
miracle tree
Will trustingly wait for
you,….yes wait

After the end of the war, Daddy's brother, Uncle Valentin, returned home, too. We rented out half of the upper portion of the house to him and Aunt Hilde until they got established. My cousin, Eberhard, was born while they lived with us. The other half was rented out to the Weiss family. This family kept on adding members. When they had four children, they lived upstairs with just a kitchen and one bedroom because they couldn't find another place to live. One day, Frau Weiss placed pieces of wood into the baking oven and closed the door while the oven was on. All of her children were in bed sleeping. She left the house to visit her mother-in-law. Since the wood and the briquettes in the oven were burning to keep the apartment warm, the wood in the baking oven didn't stay silent either. The wood got very hot and soon the entire upstairs was filled with smoke. The four sleeping children almost perished. When we started coughing and gagging downstairs, we realized that something was seriously wrong. Smoke escaped out of the locked door where the Weiss Family lived. Mama informed the fire department and ran to the mother-in-law of Frau Weiss to get Frau Weiss.

When Uncle Valentin first got home from the war, he became a salesman for Blendax toothpaste and other cosmetic items until he opened his own drugstore. Every Saturday, he took me along on his trips. I enjoyed riding in a car and seeing different places. After they had built their own home and moved to their new place, the Plume Family moved into their apartment at our house.

1949 NATO established
China becomes communist

1950 Korean War begins

Mama, Papa, and my three older sisters

ISABELL VON DER WALDESRUH

There were a few months when everything seemed to be going well for us. We enjoyed every minute living in our own home, but still much work needed to be done. As it was in those days, there was no bathroom in the house, no shower, no heating system, no telephone, just rooms. We had to go to an outhouse, even during the biting cold winters. We were accustomed to this life style because nobody knew any other way. We got our first radio when I was nine, an electric stove when I was sixteen, and a full bath when I was 22 years old. For ironing clothes, we used a flatiron by heating it on the hot stove and ironed whatever needed to be straightened out. During the very cold winters, we heated the house with wood and lignite briquettes. When I arrived home from sledding and my legs were almost frozen from the cold, I sat in front of the oven and stretched both legs into the baking oven. Mama made me KABA, the brand of the hot chocolate at that time. This warmed me up. We usually picked up the briquettes with the sled from the Guthier family who sold them and lived at the outskirts of Kirschhausen. Every year and exactly one week before Christmas Eve the schoolyard was filled with cut Christmas trees. Mama and I went early in the day, usually on a Saturday, and searched for a well-shaped, healthy looking tree which didn't lose its needles yet, loaded it on the sled, tightened it up with a rope, pulled it home, and stored it in a cool, dry place until the tree was ready to be decorated.

Every day, whether snow, rain, or sunshine, my father rode his bicycle from Kirschhausen to the train station in Heppenheim. There he caught the train to Weinheim where he worked. In the evening, when he returned home with his bicycle, he always rang the bell on his bike as soon as he opened the garden door to let everybody know that he had arrived home.

My dog, Struwwel, and I

During the summer, I was mainly outdoors with my dog, Struwwel, who was a mixed breed. His fur was mostly black with some grey in it. He also had a few curls. Struwwel always wanted to be held by me, which was so comforting. I loved him dearly. I usually sat in the front yard on the wooden bench waiting for Daddy to come home with a big smile on his face while he was ringing the bell on his bicycle. Then Struwwel and I went with Daddy inside the house. Mama had prepared the evening meal and I the youngest of the four daughters was proudly sitting right next to Daddy. He sat on one end of our long oak table, and I parked on the chair around the corner at the table right next to him. He was strict with his daughters, but also very fun loving. Giggling at the table was absolutely not allowed. We said grace before and after the meal. At times, he would say to my mother, "Mary, I hope you didn't pay too much." He was always concerned that there was not enough money for food for all of us, if mother kept on paying bills too early or too much. He wanted to make sure that there was enough money left for the rest of the month to live on. When I had turned five, I was able to read the newspaper to Daddy. He let me sit on his lap, but never said much, but I felt that he was so proud of me.

On July 19, 1950, when I was six years old, a fire broke out not far from us at the Heppenheimerstrasse at the farm and sawmill of Robert Mitsch. My father was the commander of the fire department at that time. Kirschhausen and Sonderbach arrived immediately. He also called the fire department in Heppenheim, but despite additional assistance, the barn and the stables burned down to the foundation. It was quite alarming to me to see nothing but flames. Agnes and I were in the distance sitting in the grass when all of a sudden, there was a dead mouse lying in the grass in front of me. On that same day, festivities of the annual parish fair in Kirschhausen were in full swing. It was also Mama's birthday as every year on the parish fair.

1951

May 1st was the German Labor Day and also a holiday. We took a trip once a year to Ober-Abtsteinach to the village where my mother was born and grew up. Her mother, my grandmother, lived there as well as aunts, uncles, and many cousins. It was always a feverish trip, and I do remember our last one, May 1st, 1951. We usually walked from Kirschhausen to Moerlenbach, which were about 21 kilometers. My parents knew every tiny path through the forests and every little creek that we had to jump over. My father had to carry me from time to time. It seemed that it would never rain on May 1st. Not once did we have to stay home. It was always a gorgeous day, and the birds were chirping in the trees. Sometimes we listened to a rustle in nearby leaves, maybe a deer, and the sun was shining brightly through the branches of the trees. Every year, I was all dressed up and wore on that last trip a red pleated skirt with a white, short sleeve blouse. When we arrived in Moerlenbach, we caught a slow train with a steam engine to the Kreidacher Hoehe. The train seemed to have seen better times because it was huffing and puffing through the tunnels and over the hills. I always enjoyed the train ride, but my short legs didn't like the climbing up the high stairs, which were made for grown-ups. However, I always looked forward to that train ride. It was almost the high point of the day. Of course, I was also preoccupied to see my grandmother and all the other relatives. We called our grandmother, Modda, and still call her Modda to this day, even though she no longer lives among us. When we arrived at the Kreidacher Hoehe, we had to walk another 10 kilometers to get to Ober-Abtsteinach. Seeing all the relatives, especially my grandmother, was so exciting. My mother always used this opportunity to meet with her girl friend from school when they were growing up. They shared a special closeness I cannot describe. The day went by so fast. We had an early dinner and returned back home the same way. We walked around 64 kilometers or 40 miles on that day every year. May 1st 1951 was our last trip which nobody could or would have predicted.

On February 12, **1951**, the Shah of Iran and Soraya Esfandiary-Bakhtiary had the most magnificent wedding celebration. The world had its eyes glued on Tehran,

Iran. It was for me a fascinating experience. We didn't have television, although I was able to watch it, but I do not recall from where. Maybe it was just in all the papers and magazines and I envisioned myself being there.

We were still able to play ball on the Heppenheimer Strasse, which was basically the main street in Kirschhausen. There rarely a car approaching. Aunt Agnes had a car because she owned a grocery store in Fischweiher near Heppenheim. The children from the entire neighborhood met on the street. The oldest of the children was called the leader. He divided the children into two groups and the ball was then thrown back and forth. The children at the north had to push those at the south further south and vice versa. The group who got farthest away from the start had lost.

My two close friends in the neighborhood were the sisters Ruth and Ingeborg, and their older sisters, Helma and Waltraud, were close to Marianne and Irene. When Ruth and Ingeborg stopped by at our house, we usually played outdoors with tops or balls, and when I went over to their place, sometimes alone, at other times with Agnes, we played with their huge doll house, which was well furnished.

ISABELL VON DER WALDESRUH

Once in a while, my sister Agnes and I attended a string-puppet theater in Kirschhausen, across the street from the school. Before the curtain opened, the children sang:

"Tri-tra-trullala, der Kasper, der ist wieder da." ("Tri-tra-trullala, Kasper is back again.")

Kasperle was always attacked by this grass-green alligator who assumed that he was super strong and could feed on Kasperle. However, Kasperle was much smarter. He had several tricks on hand with his fast movements like a magician and was always in control. Sometimes he gave the impression that the alligator was on top of everything. We held our breath and screamed, "Kasperle, Kasperle, Kasperle, he is behind you!" Our calling Kasperle, Kasperle made him super strong that he was able to kill the alligator with a club.

Monday, August 6, 1951, was a scorching hot day. It was also a feast day in Kirschhausen, called "Das Grosse Gebet" or "The Great Prayer". It is a form of veneration of the Holy Eucharist. This took place in our diocese since the 17th century. The faithful pray for several hours with individual prayer and prayer in community. The day ends with a festive closing hour and procession through the streets with exposition of the Holy Eucharist. Houses are decorated with candles and Christian symbols. It is also a veneration of Jesus' repose in the grave with fasting, watching, and praying to await his resurrection.

This day started like any other day. My father and I went to an early Mass at 9:00 a.m., and we knelt near the pipe organ in the upper loft. Agnes went with my mother and sat in the congregation below. Daddy had planned to go to work afterwards. My sister, Marianne, was seeing on and off Fridolin, a young man from Kirschhausen. He also knelt in the upper loft not far from my father and me. At that time, I had not received the first Eucharist yet, so only Daddy received Holy Communion. Suddenly Daddy got up and started not feeling well. He went over to Fridolin and asked him to look after me because he has to leave. When I arrived home, Daddy was throwing up in the kitchen sink and it was all green. He went over to the couch, my mother then came in and asked Daddy what is wrong, but he just groaned, then his eyes rolled to the side, and he was gone. My mother screamed, "Hans!" but no response. On Mondays, Dr. Berg, our family doctor, visited patients at the Villa Rosemary, which was a two minute walk from our house. When Daddy got home from church on this particular day, he saw the doctor and waved at him to come in and see him. Dr. Berg didn't realize the urgency and saw the other patients first. My mother instructed Agnes to run to the Villa Rosemary to get Dr. Berg. When Mama saw Dr. Berg coming toward our house, she yelled at him,

"Hurry!" Dr. Berg stepped into the kitchen, saw my father lying motionless on the couch, he called out, "O my God, I think it is too late!" He still gave him an injection into the heart, but my father no longer responded to it. He was gone. He was only 43 years old. My mother was the same age. This all took place in my presence when I was seven years old. I did not understand what was going on.

Strange things happened in the eyes of a seven-year-old child, who was me. Marianne and Irene were called at work to come home. Daddy's mother, Grandmother Barbara, came to the house crying. Everyone who came wore black clothes and was crying. Why are all these people crying? I thought. There was also a deadly silence at the same time. Then they carried Daddy into the living room and placed him there on the couch. One of those present had asked the local butcher to bring big ice blocks, which they placed under the couch. I heard them talking because of the high temperatures outside. I wondered what all this meant. When my sisters arrived home, Mama just said to us, "Euer Papa…" or "Your Daddy…" I still didn't understand. Grandmother Barbara said, "I still wanted to tell him so much." She died ten months later after my father on June 6, 1952. I never saw my mother smile again. At my Daddy's funeral, I held a bouquet of forget-me-nots in my hand. I was instructed to throw them into the grave when I was told to do so. I had wrapped a hand-kerchief around the stems. When Uncle Gregor tipped my arm to throw the flowers into the grave, I forgot to take off the handkerchief and threw it down into that deep hole with the flowers. When I realized what I had done, I cried so much. I wanted this handkerchief back. Uncle Gregor tried to soothe me, but I wanted my handkerchief back. He then gave me his own. This settled me down. My Daddy did not return and something was ripped out of me.

I just had started second grade and was an excellent student. After my father's death, I was unable to fall asleep at night. My mother in her deep sorrow got alarmed and talked to Dr. Berg. He prescribed sleep-ing pills for me to take. Shortly after, my mother ap-proached the doctor again and told him, "A child has to sleep and should not be on sleeping pills." My mother was grieving so much that I couldn't talk to her. I didn't want to burden her. She cried a lot. My health condition didn't change. The sleeping problem was now ongoing. My grades dropped, and I used to be a top student who loved school and studying. Soon after, I started having absence seizures. I just dropped the things I held in my hand. Sometimes I was unable to continue a conversation, at other times I lost my train of thought completely. They became more and more frequent. My illness added to my mother's many concerns. Sometimes I was just rubbing my eyes. It seemed that I was very tired, but it was just the precursor of an absence seizure. Then I had hundreds a day. My mother took me to Dr. Schlapp, a neurologist in Heppenheim. It was a nightmare for my mother because in those days, medication or the correct diagnosis was not readily available.

Mama decided that I should spend a few weeks with her mother in Ober-Abtsteinach and all my aunts, uncles, and cousins, to get some fresh air and get somewhat distracted from all the recent happening in my young life. Modda taught me the following prayer, since I slept with her in the same bed.

Abendgebet	Evening prayer
Abends wenn ich schlafen geh	In the evening when I go to bed
Vierzehn Engel bei mir stehn	Fourteen angels stand around me
Zwei zu meiner Rechten	Two at my right
Zwei zu meiner Linken	Two at my left
Zwei zu meinen Haeupten	Two at my head
Zwei zu meinen Fuessen	Two at my feet
Zwei die mich decken	Two who cover me
Zwei die mich wecken	Two who awaken me

| Zwei die mich weisen | Two who show me the way |
| In das himmlische Paradeischen | To the heavenly paradise |

I was quite upset and wanted to go home again. I wrote a letter to Mama and told her that she sent me to Ober-Abtsteinach because she doesn't want me anymore. I didn't know how to mail the letter. Modda got a hold of my little wrapped package. She informed Mama who tried to convince me that she loved me by explaining to me that a stay in Ober-Abtsteinach with Modda and other family members could help me to get over the loss of Papa. I stayed and adjusted somewhat. We played games in the evening. Most of all, I liked when Modda used the butter churn and made butter. After a while, the tiled stove next to the couch instilled in me a homey feeling. When we played cards or board games in the evening with Franz, Marianne, and Modda, I forgot that I wanted to go home. I also played with my other cousins, Marga and Leni. Marga introduced me to her classmates who were all my age. I was also allowed to attend classes with Marga. Teaching was more like play, which didn't seem to be the case in Kirschhausen. In the evening before dark, Marga and I walked with an empty tin can to a farm called *Windhof* and picked up fresh milk. Life in Ober-Abtsteinach was more relaxed than life in Kirschhausen. Ober-Abtsteinach was much more country like at that time while Kirschhausen close to the city of Heppenheim had more the flavor of a small town, even there used to be many farmers in Kirschhausen. When my cousin, Franz, turned 17, he got killed on Fastnacht (Mardi Gras) in an automobile accident. It was a distressing time for Modda, since she raised her grandchildren while Uncle Franz and Aunt Eva worked in the fields.

1952   Elizabeth becomes queen

My First Holy Communion in 1952

One week after Easter, April 20, 1952, and one year after my father's death, I received my First Holy Communion. As it was the custom in those days, you needed another child close to your age who already had received the First Holy Communion to hold your big candle while you received for the first time. My sister, Agnes, was my candle holder. It was another sad day for my mother. Photos reveal how she felt. I received many gifts, beautifully decorated coffee cups, handkerchiefs that I have kept to this day, and many monetary gifts, which I gave to my mother to use where she saw fit. At 6:00 p.m., our priest, Pfarrer Wolf, went with the children who had received their First Holy Communion to the cemetery in Kirschhausen. When I saw my father's grave on this very special day in my life, my thoughts and feelings were torn apart. Joy and sorrow didn't know how to look into each other's face. I was only eight years old.

My mother was very strict when it came to our faith. I was expected to go to confession every other week. As it was in those days, we had to write our sins down. Mama would read them. I have the feeling that she did this to find out whether I understood what a sin was. I really was afraid that everything was a sin, and I didn't quite know the difference between forgetfulness and sin. Looking back at those times, I have a strong feeling that Mama had great anxieties. She had to raise her four children alone without the strong hand of a father.

ISABELL VON DER WALDESRUH

She wanted to make sure that we would become good and decent people. She loved her faith, but she could have been also somewhat depressed. The burden she had to carry was quite heavy for her.

My school had arranged a trip to the circus in Bensheim to see the Ringling Brothers Barnum & Bailey. My mother didn't have the money to let me go with the school. My second grade teacher, Fraeulein Schachner, paid for my trip. This was an unforgettable experience. My greatest memory of this event is how the baby elephants walked in a big circle, their trunk holding on to the tail of the other baby elephant in front. This was the very first time I ever saw an elephant. I'm forever grateful to Fraeulein Schachner for this experience.

Because of my ongoing condition, many mornings I was very sleepy and not really present. My hands dropped while holding the hot chocolate. The neurologist had instructed Mama to place me on the couch immediately until I was fine again. Therefore, I missed on and off the first two hours of school or an entire day. Mama had always tear-dimmed eyes after I had an episode. In the afternoon, after I had completed my homework, Mama insisted that I rest on the couch for a while. I followed her advice. Her opinion was that a brain needs some rest after studying, especially considering my condition. By that time, we had acquired a radio. In the afternoon they broadcasted lessons designed for students and young children. I was always eager to learn new things and it didn't matter what the subject was. Because of my chronic illness, I had missed many hours of school. From these programs I learned things they did not teach in school. I remember clearly when I learned about the Eder dam. The Eder Dam is a hydroelectric dam spanning the Eder River from northern Hesse, Germany. The dam was breached in World War II by bouncing bombs dropped by British Lancaster bombers. The dam was rebuilt by forced labor drawn from construction of the Atlantic Wall under command of Organisation Todt.

My cousin, Gerda, was afflicted with asthma and her doctor prescribed six weeks of convalescence for her in Wyk auf Foehr at the North Sea. She suffered greatly under homesickness. It was almost necessary to break up her stay. Agnes and I wrote Gerda a letter and placed Struwwel's paw prints on the letter. This cheered her up, and she decided to stay until her discharge, as she had mentioned on her arrival back home.

Gerda spent a lot of time at our house because her mother worked outside the home. She was the sole bread winner. We played openly in our yard. One afternoon, One afternoon, Gerda and I were sitting in the front yard on the wooden bench inspecting each other, as I assume all little girls do. My mother caught us and told me that she would let Papa know about it. I felt guilty but wasn't sure why.

My street, Honerbachstrasse, fell sharply toward the main street. I always rushed down the street and wouldn't settle for walking. The street had no asphalt and my running caused me several times to nosedive and have open bleeding knees from all the sand and the pebbles. Mama always advised me not to run. I listened to her, but forgot it as soon as I had closed the door behind me.

As time went on, my life took on a different dimension, and I was sad because of what I had to go through. I began worrying about my future. However, I always smiled as my childhood pictures reveal.

June 2, **1953**, the world watched the coronation of Queen Elizabeth II as monarch of the United Kingdom, Canada, Australia, New Zealand, South Africa, Pakistan, and Ceylon.

One winter, it was so bitter cold that the water in the pipes in our cellar froze where we had stored our potatoes. Mama was so afraid that the pipes would break. Frau Weiss's brother-in-law, Herr Abramowic, who spoke with a strong Polish accent, was called. He walked along the pipe with a burning stick and tried to melt the ice. Mama had to endure a lot of anxiety. I'm sure that she cried often. My father was no longer around and everything depended on her. What will happen if the pipe breaks? A big boiler and a huge bathtub were located in a nearby room where Mama washed our clothes and we took a bath. After a long time and with a lot of worrying and praying, the ice lost its grip and the water was flowing again.

1953   Mt. Everest climbed for the first time
DNA discovered
Stalin dies

A major flood arose in August of 1953 in Kirschhausen. The Heppenheimerstrasse, the main street, was filled with water about 28 inches high. The firefighters had a very difficult time not getting swept away with the current. The water was all the way up to the rim of their boots. The creek that ran next to our garden which was adjacent to the house turned into a raging river. It took along our entire garden, vegetables, flowers, and all, just left the house standing. The rain continued to hammer on our roof. My mother, a woman of faith, lit a candle in the living-room as nightfall was close at hand and sat there in silence. That was all she was able to do. Yet she never gave up. Her life was not an easy one. Raising four children without a husband, her youngest daughter had a continuous illness, and every penny needed to be turned twice that she wouldn't spend too much. The house needed to be rendered, which is mainly a man's job.

Throughout the summer we removed beetles from our potato plants. We harvested the potatoes in the fall, and at the end of the season, we burned the vines. We had fun roasting potatoes in the crackling campfire. We sang songs, and Struwwel enjoyed running in circles, digging holes, and sniffing all these various smells in the ground.

Every month, my mother had a few religious magazines coming to the house. Agnes distributed them to other families who had subscribed to them. I scanned through the pictures and read about the lives of other cultures. Their different looks and expressions as well as their needs, physically and spiritually, impressed me quite a bit. It was my great wish to become a missionary to Japan, to live among the native people. I thought that somehow dreams can become reality.

1954   First atomic submarine launched
The Soccer World Cup took place in Bern, Switzerland, from 16 June – 4 July **1954**. Germany won the World Cup. The celebration went on forever and the Germans displayed a great sense of pride.

I continued to have multiple absence seizures a day and was referred to the clinic at the University of Heidelberg. Whenever I had an appointment, they conducted an

EEG (electroencephalogram) and lab work because I took medication. My treating physicians had become father figures to me. They were all nice, caring, and smart, like Papa. They gave me their full attention, and I loved to go to Heidelberg. In 1954, I had to stay in Heidelberg for a few weeks for observation. Other children with various issues were there, too. We also had lessons during the day. I stayed over Easter and received a big chocolate rabbit for being so studious. I enjoyed the huge playground with the swing, which I didn't have at home. Despite my condition, I was allowed to use the swing. After being there for nine days, I got a major seizure and was transferred to another clinic. I got so upset when I was lying in bed and staring at those white walls. There was no other patient with me in the room. The door to my room was open and I saw only adult patients walk by. I cried so much and begged the doctors to let me return to the clinic at the Blumenstrasse, to the children, and to the swing. They reconsidered my wish and allowed me to transfer back. The following Sunday, Marianne visited me with Fridolin, her current boyfriend, at the children's clinic. We walked up to the Heidelberg Castle. I was so at awe by its ruins, the view of the city from above, and the Neckar River snaking through the landscape was quite impressive, too. I had fallen in love with Heidelberg much earlier. It had become my second home. When I got discharged from the clinic, my condition was somewhat controlled, but medications for a seizure disorder in 1954 were still very limited. They also had many alarming side effects, like teeth falling out or when walking outdoors, everything appeared to be milky or snow-white. Therefore, the medication needed to be changed often.

Many asked and so did I at that very young age: What are seizures or Epilepsy? Seizures or Epilepsy is a complex disease. Epilepsy is a Greek word and means "falling sickness." The emperor Napoleon and the statesman Caesar both suffered from Epilepsy. Millions of people worldwide are afflicted with this disease.

When a person suffers from Epilepsy, the brain gives out electrical impulses. He may drop his fork or spoon while eating, or stop talking in the middle of a sentence. Often, he does not remember where he left off. Some stare at one spot; roll the eyes; or just daydream.

Another seizure, which actually looks serious, is when a person falls unexpectedly to the ground and loses consciousness. He makes twisting movements with his arms and legs. These are called tonic-clonic seizures. They are very exhausting that the person sleeps for several hours afterwards. Some experience a sensation or warning before a seizure, called *aura*. This can prevent the person from falling because he can go quickly to a safe place. Not all people with epileptic seizures experience an *aura*.

The disease is not contagious, and the people are not mentally ill. They have an average to high intelligence, attend school, and compete in sports. Many are involved in extra school programs, play the piano and other instruments. Hamburgers and French fries are one of their favorite foods, too. However, they must eat healthy, balanced meals, like you and me, with lots of vitamins and minerals. These nourish the brain.

Most seizures start at an early age. The pediatrician, a doctor who treats childhood illnesses, refers the patient to a neurologist. This is a doctor who treats diseases of the nerves. The doctor performs a physical and a neurological exam, to find out the nature of the disease. He writes down the patient's past and his family's medical history. He orders an EEG, called electroencephalogram. The device, called electroencephalograph, consists of electrodes and an electronic amplifying system. The EEG technician places the electrodes over the skin on the top and back of the head of the patient. This test doesn't hurt. The EEG records the brain waves and shows any disorders. These are very important to the doctor for his diagnosis. It also informs him which section of the brain sparks the abnormal electrical impulses or so-called seizures.

Some seizures are caused by injuries to the brain. If these injuries form scar tissue, this can prompt seizures, too. Tumors of the brain, disturbances in blood

ISABELL VON DER WALDESRUH

circulation to the brain, infections, and other reasons can cause seizures. Diseases affecting the brain received from ones ancestors may be another factor. In 70% of cases, no known cause is ever found.

Most major seizures last only a minute or two and require little of the bystander. The seizure needs to run its course. Now and then a person does not recover consciousness. This is life threatening. Someone needs to call 911 or an emergency unit immediately.

If you see a person having a seizure, don't become frightened. Keep him safe. Remove sharp objects that he cannot hurt himself. Place a pillow under his head. If you can, turn the person to the side that the saliva flows out. Do not put anything into his mouth. He may feel weak or confused after the seizure and need help getting home.

The doctor generally tries several medications before the patient responds to one. Two, three or even more tablets must be taken daily and at the same hour. Medication is the most common treatment of Epilepsy. The patient has to follow his doctor's instructions to remain free of seizures. He must never stop taking the medication on his own. Getting at least eight hours of sleep every night is important because the brain needs plenty of rest. When a child stays seizure-free, he is permitted to swim, ride his bike, participate in sports, and later on to drive a car.

Drinking alcohol can increase seizure activity. Therefore, it is wise to avoid it. Besides, alcohol disagrees with nearly all medications.

Most people with Epilepsy wear a bracelet or necklace with a tag. This tag informs others that its wearer has a medical condition. An emergency phone number is engraved in it. The other side of the tag shows a serpent, which is a medical symbol.

A medical cure for this complex disease has not been found yet. Scientists, doctors, and nurses are working tirelessly to find one. People with seizures (maybe you know someone) don't want to be looked at as different or be shunned. They are just ordinary people who live with Epilepsy.

After Christmas, usually on January 3rd, my birthday, Mama and I took the bus to Heppenheim, then the train to Weinheim, and from there we continued on with a bus to Ober-Abtsteinach to see my mother's mother and the rest of the family. Modda was a great comfort and support to Mama after Papa had died. I remember that on my 10th birthday, I received an orange from my Grandmother Maria or Modda, as we called her. This was the first orange in my life, and now we take oranges for granted. She also used to come to Kirschhausen every summer for three months and assisted Mama with all the work in the garden. We harvested the green beans. Modda would slice them, which was an enormous task. They were placed in a clean, large stoneware pot in the order of two inches green beans and then a thick layer of salt and continued in that order until the stoneware pot was full. Some savory was added on and off. The last layer was salt. It was covered with cloth and a heavy weight. After 6 – 8 weeks the green beans were ready to eat, but we waited a little longer. Since we made always a generous amount of the green beans, we carried a large bowl full to the Sisters as long as they stayed in Kirschhausen. We always looked forward to Modda's coming. It was hard on Mama when she left. She had to fight with her tears but some escaped.

1955

For the third time in 50 years, my parish, St. Bartholomew in Kirschhausen, had to order new church bells under great financial sacrifices. On January 10, 1942, the two biggest bells had been confiscated for military purposes. We received our new church bells on May 19, 1955, on the feast of the Ascension of Christ. They were blessed by Vicar General Kastell. I still see those three mighty church bells standing next to each other on a huge wooden frame at the church square. The largest bell weighed 845 kg, the second one 600 kg, and the smallest one 355 kg. Each one had a different inscription. Some parishioners even viewed this awesome happening of the casting of the bells.

In 1955, my mother took me to an investiture of a nun. She was a young woman from Kirschhausen. Mama thought that this would be an important experience for me because I had not abandoned my missionary plans. We boarded the bus before 6:00 a.m. and drove for about three hours to Ellwangen on the Jagst River. The service started at 9:00 a.m. I was the only child with a bus full of adults. It was a somewhat strange experience for me. The ceremony took another three hours. I was so bored because most of the various symbolic happenings had no meaning to me. I was looking forward to lunch and chose spaghetti and tomato sauce. We still had some time left after lunch for some sight-seeing before returning home. We visited the pilgrimage church Schoenenberg with the newly vested Sister. Mama purchased a souvenir for me, which was a little white flower and could be worn on a chain. When you looked through a tiny hole in the heart of the flower, you saw the picture of the pilgrimage church Schoenenberg. I still have it after so many years. My son or my grandchildren do not know anything about it until they read it here.

I'm with my three older sisters. I was about age 8 or 9

In 1955, quite a few weddings were going on. My cousin, Leni, from Ober Abtsteinach got married to Werner Kohl from Ober-Flockenbach, and my cousin, Roesl, from Lorsch got married to Hans Bierbaum from Lorsch. Both had planned huge weddings and basically everybody was invited, as it seemed to me. Since there were many children like myself, in the evening we were placed in reserved rooms at their house with pillows and blankets right on the carpeted floor and next to each other. It was fun and something totally new to me. Most of the children I had never met. I knew only Marga from Ober-Abtsteinach. An adult checked on us from time to time. Going home that evening was impossible. There were no more busses running, but I was glad.

1956 Suez Crisis
       Hungarian Revolution

On April 19, 1956, the American actress Grace Patricia Kelly married at Monaco's Saint Nicholas Cathedral Prince Rainier III of Monaco. I watched this pure romance in black and white on Fridolin's television, but it was still glamorous.

As children we jumped ropes or did Double Dutch. At Easter, we asked the owner of Villa Rosemary, Frau Honerbach, whether we could use the hillside next to her house for rolling our Easter eggs. The property belonged to her, but she was not a generous woman. To our surprise, she answered us with a big YES. We all thanked her.

My mother opened part of our house to guests who vacationed at Villa Rosemary. Kirschhausen is a climatic health-resort and many people sought the healthy and fresh air almost all year around. Guests had their meals at Villa Rosemary, but they slept at our house. Mama had a toiletry set out of stoneware for our guest. There was a time during the summer when young people chose to stay with us because there were young people at our house, too. It also brought some distraction into my mother's life as well as income. She also made new friends who shared with her their life. When Papa was still alive, Mama was sometimes jealous of Papa when he talked with guests from Villa Rosemary when they walked by at our house.

When Agnes had switched over to a school with higher learning in Heppenheim, she was directed to memorize English vocabulary. This gave me the chance to study along with her. Later on, I was unable to attend the same school because of my health issues. I would have missed too many classes. This was so difficult for me to accept. I didn't know at that time how hard this would be for me in later life.

I had to go to bed in the evening much sooner than my older sisters. Mama was so concerned that she made sure that I get at least eight to nine hours of sleep. One evening, an idea popped into my head. A white curtain hung in front of the window in our bedroom. The Heppenheimerstrasse was fully lit. The street light shone toward the bedroom window and the closed curtain. I envisioned that in order to stay up a little longer and to the same degree as my sisters, I must play a trick. I drew a hand on plain paper, cut it out, and pinned it to the outside of the curtain. The shadow of the hand looked really cool from the inside. I didn't say anything to my sisters. When my mother said, "Rita, it is bedtime!" I got undressed and put on my flowery nightgown. When Mama walked with me into the bedroom, I cried out, "There is someone climbing up the window!" Mama looked at the window and noticed the shadow, but she said calmly, "Well, that is one of the flower pots." There were no flower pots on that window. She hesitantly walked over to the window and detected my pinned on hand. I then had some explaining to do. Mama allowed me after this incident to stay up a little longer. I had accomplished what I initially wanted, to stay up longer, but it was only half an hour.

Gerda, the one who had asthma, I have two cousins with the name Gerda, also always participated in the Easter egg hunt. During the war, many girls were named

Gerda because Adolf Hitler liked that name. Gerda and her mother, my father's sister and my Godmother, lived close by. They had rented an apartment from Frau Schaefer who had three cats. Gerda had a green doll carriage. She dressed up the cats and forced all three to sit in her doll carriage. The cats didn't like to be confined and meowed a lot. Frau Schaefer always said to Gerda in an angry voice, "Des Katze Gedalk!" ("This tormenting of the cats!") She objected strongly to this handling of the cats, but didn't do anything about it.

My classmate and friend, Christel, stopped by every afternoon after she was finished with homework. My mother and her mother had become friends, too. They had things in common and both were widows. My mother didn't have it easy in Kirschhausen, especially in the beginning. She was looked at as somewhat inferior. My father came from a very large farm and my mother from a small one. Having a friend who was in a somewhat similar situation helped her to overcome some hurdles.

Karin, my other classmate and friend, was the daughter of our forest ranger and my neighbor. Every year, she threw an enjoyable birthday party and invited all the other classmates. However, we were only a small group because of the war. Karin always excused herself for her bad grade in German because her mother was Dutch.

Birthday party – I sit next to the birthday girl with the ball.
My hair is braided on top.

Mama had a mortgage to pay, but there was no longer an income. She received only a minimum of half-orphan pensions for the four of us and a tiny widow pension for herself. This was basically the only monthly income. She had to find other means, like renting out a room to the Villa Rosemary. Much still needed to be done on our house that could be only accomplished with man power and money. Marianne and Irene had to leave their apprenticeship and work full time with regular pay. Agnes needed four more years of schooling to reach the same educational level that Marianne and Irene had reached. Marianne and Irene worked for the same company our father worked for. Agnes joined them after her graduation.

The season of Advent was an exciting waiting period. Marianne and I went to the Weber's Heck into the forest and cut off some fir branches for the Advent wreath. Nobody would have said anything for cutting off a few branches. Karin, my classmate and neighbor, her father was the forest ranger, would not have punished us in any way if he would have caught us for cutting off a few branches for an Advent wreath. At home, Marianne positioned the branches around a wire, placed four red candles on the finished wreath, and wrapped a red ribbon around it. We sang Advent songs and hoped to get from Mama some freshly baked Christmas cookies. Sometimes she allowed us to help her cutting out the dough with the cookie cutters. The time of waiting for Christmas, like in Old Testament times, was almost relived.

Christmas was always very difficult for all of us without Papa. On Christmas Eve, we usually had a simple meal that consisted of cooked red beets or red beet salad, roasted potatoes, and roasted blood sausage. Blood sausage is my most favorite sausage to this day, especially when roasted in the pan. Mama had decorated the tree in the living-room in the afternoon, as she did every year. No one was allowed to enter. One year, she surprised us with a nativity scene. She then added every year a new shepherd, a wise man, and so on until it was complete. Hans Bierbaum, the husband of my cousin Roesl, made us a shed. When Mama permitted us to enter the living-room, we then role played the song *Seeking Shelter*, an Austrian song. The pregnant Mary and Joseph were looking for a place to stay, but they were turned away until they found a barn where the Baby Jesus was born. Then we lit some sparklers. It was a very festive atmosphere and the fragrance of the fir tree, the flickering of the burning candles, and the aroma of the Christmas cookies made everything so special. Mama's anise cookies used to be my favorite. The flavor was close to licorice, also my best loved candy, but it was not always available. I also loved to drink fennel tea, which also tasted like anise. We continued Christmas Eve with prayer, sang Christmas songs, and then Mama handed out the presents. I still remember how thrilled I was when I got a blue sewing machine so that I could sew the clothes for my dolls. I tried to figure out almost immediately how it worked.

Most Christmases during my childhood were quite cold and the ground was usually packed with snow. We always had ice flowers on our windows, since the rooms were not heated. We slept in cold bedrooms, and only the living-room and the kitchen had a stove. On Christmas Day, we all went to the Midnight Mass, which started at 4:00 a.m. Because of the excitement on Christmas Eve, I was ill frequently on Christmas Day and had to stay in bed because I was unresponsive. Any excitement was never good for me, whether it was joy or sorrow. I assume that my nervous system was not developed enough to handle any emotions.

Marianne displayed great talents in sewing, and Irene was creative with cooking. On weekends, Marianne sewed all our dresses and costumes. We also owned a knitting machine. With this machine, she knitted all our sweaters. Irene cooked the meals on weekends. This was a break for Mama, and Irene enjoyed it very much. We always worked as a team.

My future brother-in-law, Fridolin, was the second person in Kirschhausen who had purchased a television. It was only in black and white at that time. However, I was allowed to watch children's programs. His mother, a sweet, white-haired, elderly lady always turned it on and off for me.

1957   Space Age begins

In Kirschhausen lived a woman who was from Belarus. I don't know whether her mother tongue was Russian or Belarus. While she lived outside of Kirschhausen in the forest with her grown son, she traveled to Kirschhausen to do grocery shopping. She spoke a strange German dialect. She knew that Gerda laughed about her and her dialect. I don't recall that I said anything to Frau Drechsler that was upsetting her, but she always said to us in her dialect, "Ultra Leit uslacha" in German "Alte Leute auslachen" ("laugh at old people").

Every spring, Agnes and I went out in the meadow near the Weber's Heck and picked cowslips. These awesome, yellow spring flowers which usually bloom from March to May or June have an aromatic and pleasant scent. They almost smelled like a fresh apricot. The roots have also been used for healing purposes. During May we decorated one room of the house with cowslips in honor of the Blessed Mother. My three sisters and I took long walks in the forest, also sang songs, and brought tree branches home with the leaves still attached to them. We placed those in large vases filled with water and decorated the inside of the house. Living with nature in the house instilled a feeling of well-being.

When Marianne married Fridolin on May 1st, 1957, I felt abandoned. From infancy on, she was always very close to me. I had shared with her a different closeness than I did with my mother or my other sisters. She had a big wedding, and there were many children to play with. The food was less important to me, but my world had changed. I lost my big sister to someone else. I couldn't keep her back home. She was still my big sister, and I noticed that Mama's face displayed some sadness as well. Marianne continued to live in Kirschhausen, but someone else was now in first place. I thought life must be that way that you have many disappointments and pain.

When I was in third grade, I had Frau Frank as my teacher. She always handed me a jar filled with honey. She thought that would strengthen me. I always was a little upset that other children whose father had never returned from the war received free meals with hot chocolate during school hours. My father probably died from the gunshot wound in his arm, which was the result of the war. He still had shrapnel in his right arm. I had to accept that, but I would have loved to have a cup of hot chocolate while at school, too. I was not envious of my classmate and friend, Margot. Her father didn't return. She also had no brothers or sisters.

Frau Frank had a wonderful ritual during the Advent season, the time before Christmas. She carried many pieces of straw to class. On each piece was a golden dot. We received a straw with a golden dot when we behaved during lessons. The student that had collected the most straws by Christmas was allowed to lay the Baby Jesus into the crib. I do not recall that I was that lucky because I was at times quite restless and couldn't sit still.

I loved the snow when I was a child. This meant sledding with Christel. Many hills surround Kirschhausen. But there was a lot of walking involved, too. A march back with the sled to the beginning of the toboggan run took about 10 – 15 minutes. Many times I used the belly flop position, which I greatly enjoyed. On days when I went sledding without Christel, I took a rope and placed Struwwel in front of the sled. We rode down Heppenheimer Strasse. When the speed increased too much, I called on Struwwel to slow down. The continuously increasing speed could have flung me off. Almost nobody owned a car yet. The doctor and only a few well off people enjoyed that luxury. Later on, it was no longer possible to use the main street.

I'm tired from sledding

Christel and I went deep into the forest and collected wood. We had such a big load that it took us forever to get home. We arrived at our house when it was pitch dark. It was a big mistake on my part that I worked so hard because it affected my brain and I got a seizure. To top it off, Mama was waiting at home with excruciating pain in her stomach. After Dr. Ferarri had examined her, she was rushed to the hospital and was diagnosed with a busted appendix. Her entire abdomen was full of pus, and we almost lost her at that time. Her mother was called upon, and she stayed with us the entire time. There was a lot to do. The pig needed to be fed, and someone needed to be at the house. My three older sisters had responsible positions at the company Carl Freudenberg. Marianne had just gotten married and no longer lived at home. During Mama's stay in the hospital, I missed her so much that I had symptoms of appendicitis, too, and I was admitted to the hospital. They removed my appendix at that time.

1958   Mao Zedong launches Great Leap Forward

Christel lived on the other side of the Heppenheimer Strasse (main street). To walk to the forest from her house took only a few minutes. Near this forest was a site my sisters and I called the Schlonge huul (snake den). All the boys met there and some girls. I just watched them from time to time, but never participated. They used to dress like Indians and had their faces painted yellow and red. The boys were swinging on hanging tree branches and made strange noises. I always told Christel, "This is not my thing. I do not want to participate ever."

After a few years renting out our left upstairs, Herr and Frau Plume moved to their daughter's home. Soon afterwards, Mama found in the attic a loaded weapon. This shocked her greatly, especially since Papa was no longer alive. Herr and Frau Plume and their two daughters were refugees from the war. They fled from the Sudetenland, the German speaking part of Czechoslovakia. Mama had second thoughts when it came to Herr Plume. She felt uneasy, concerned, and assumed that he had left it there. We never found out whose weapon it was.

After the war, schools had basically no books or any other teaching material. For first and second grade, we wrote on the same slate with the same pen. It was easy to clean. Penmanship was very important. We had wooden folding desks with two flip-up seats. When we got called to the front, we had to step out on the side. On the right side of the desk was a built-in inkpot. I remember an incident like it just had happened yesterday. I was in second grade and learned about George Washington. It was a big foreign name to me. We had to write two to three sentences about him. I sat in my bench and kept on saying the word Was-hing-ton, Was-hing-ton, Was-hing-ton. When I wrote my sentences, I got it all right.

Later on, when I was in 4th and 5th grade, my teacher, Herr Nack, requested from his students that we purchase *The Tellusbogen*, which was a monthly magazine. Every little thing that cost money was hard on my mother's purse. In later years, and when Lehrer Kohl was our teacher until 8th grade, we had only one book to read and it belonged to the school. Also, 6th, 7th, and 8th grade were taught together in one room. Some children were quite disrespectful toward Herr Kohl. He was close to retirement. When he got very excited, he was spitting while talking to us students. Some kids told him, "We need an umbrella!"

I listened a lot to music and knew the latest sellouts. "*The legionnaire*" and "*Homeless*", sung by Freddy Quinn, "*Where my sun is shining*" by Caterina Valente, "*The laughing vagabond*" by Fred Bertelman, and the "*River Kwai March*" by Mitch Miller. Freddy sang also many shanties. I often walked over to the stairs leading upwards and called Frau Weiss when I heard Freddy first before she had turned on the radio. She loved his songs, too. I think everybody at that time did. He brought freshness and new ideas into the people's lives after the war.

During my years at school, teachers remained silent about the war and didn't inform us what actually happened. Either they were ashamed and didn't want to talk about it, or they didn't know much or anything at all. I sometimes asked Mama about the Jewish people and what she knew because she had Jewish friends. Also a synagogue existed in Heppenheim. She used to work in Heppenheim before she married my father. Her answer was that they were told that the Jewish people were transferred to a working camp.

Uncle Franz, the beekeeper, had many beehives. Since he lived next to our property near the creek that separated us, his bees always swarmed over to our side. One afternoon, while I was picking plums from our plum tree, I got stung by a swarm of bees on the top of my head. I got so frightened and screamed because they wouldn't get out of my hair.

My best friend, Christel, and I loved to go together into the deep forest to collect mushrooms. It took us usually three hours until we returned back home again. She knew the difference between poisonous and edible mushrooms better than I did. My favorite ones were porcinis and chanterelles. Mama was acquainted with many recipes. My best-loved recipe was sliced champignons with pasta. I still use it today. Chanterelles are

ISABELL VON DER WALDESRUH

not always available in grocery stores: however, they may be available in specialty stores.

Champignons with pasta:

You will need:
300g pork, sliced
300g champignons, sliced
Salt, pepper
1 onion, chopped
2 tsp mustard
1 Tbsp flour
1 c beef broth
1/2 c sour cream
Parsley, chopped

Slice meat and champignons, add pepper and salt
Chop onion and brown in hot margarine, add mushrooms and meat
Add mustard and flour
Add beef broth and stir. Cook 20 minutes on low heat
Add sour cream and chopped parsley

Mama was quite inventive. Her organizational skills were enormous. We had an acre of land with our house. About two-third was used for potatoes. The rest was grass, and a plum and an apple tree decorated this piece. The plums and the apples that grew there were used for marmalade. Some apples Mama stored for eating. She also baked quite a few plum cakes.

Next to Uncle Franz, the beekeeper, lived the Polzer Family who raised rabbits. One day, Herr Polzer asked Mama whether his rabbits could feed on our grass. My mother permitted it under one condition that in return we would receive a rabbit for a meal occasionally. The deal was made, and every other month, Mama prepared a rabbit for our Sunday dinner.

One day, Mama cut grass with a sickle. She was so busy getting her work done when she suddenly felt sogginess in her left shoe. She got very scared when she realized that the inside of her left shoe was filling up with blood. She immediately rushed to the house and, thank God, Irene was home who secured her artery. She also notified Dr. Berg who arrived at our house in less than ten minutes.

In 1958, I graduated from the Volksschule in Kirschhausen. Christel started working in Heppenheim for a company who makes umbrellas. I was not yet able to ride the bus to Heppenheim because my condition was not under control yet. I stayed home and helped Mama around the house and learned cooking. I taught myself shorthand and typing. My older sisters, especially Irene, tested me from time to time. As a start, Aunt Margret and Aunt

Agnes offered me a part time job at their grocery store in Kirschhausen. They paid me some pocket money. I was shy of customers because I was afraid I would get an absence seizure. Therefore, I was not very outgoing. I stayed only a few months.

On February 6, 1958, Marianne and Fridolin became parents to a little boy. As soon as the weather got warmer, Marianne entrusted little Peter to me for walks with the baby carriage in Kirschhausen. I adored my first nephew very much, and every afternoon at 3:00 p.m., I was there for a walk with that little boy.

In the fall, I was admitted to the clinic in Heidelberg for a trial with a newer medication. At that time, the university hospitals were mainly staffed by nuns. During my stay, the Papal conclave occurred following the death of Pope Pius XII on 9 October 1958 in Castel Gandolfo, after a 19-year pontificate. The ward Sister turned on the radio for the patients who wanted to listen to it. As a patient at the University Clinic, my case was teaching material for medical students. I was called by the professor to appear in front of at least 100 students. I got so nervous when I saw these young men and women scrutinizing me. The professor had a comforting expression. I had met him before. Dr. Hollaender notified me not to worry about. Soon I learned that it was no question and answer session.

I was just asked to count to 100. This was not hard to do. I was still a little nervous. I do not remember whether an absence seizure occurred or not. After my stay in Heidelberg, I continued to see my physician as an outpatient. After the appointment, Mama and I had lunch and usually strolled along the banks of the Neckar River. We closed the day in Heidelberg with some shopping. The train and bus rides were covered for both of us by the health insurance.

Also in 1958, Aunt Katie arrived from South Africa with two of her children and stayed for nine months. They lived in Ober-Abtsteinach with Modda. Jeanette turned 18 while in Germany and Peter was five. They visited us in Kirschhausen, too. Jeanette and Peter spoke some German. Since we didn't have a full bath at that time, little Peter said in his limited German, "Ihr seid Sau, Ihr tut nicht baden!" ("You are pigs, you don't bathe!") Jeanette, Agnes, and I walked all the way to the Starkenburg Castle. On the way up, we chose tree-covered trails, and Jeanette engraved her name into the bark of one of the trees. When we reached the top near the castle, the view of the Rhine valley was awesome. It was a clear day, and for Jeanette, coming from South Africa, it was most likely a fascinating experience to be able to view the entire area north, south, east, and west. Each direction presented a different, attractive, natural scenery. I'm sure that she was proud that Germany was the birthplace of her mother. The ruins reminded all of us of battles fought long time ago. The Romans were already using this place's strategic location, in which they built a fort. The Roman fortification of the heights was a forerunner to the later castle. The complex is believed to have been destroyed by the Franks about 412.

Mama raised a pig. Every year we held a Schlachtfest (slaughter of a pig with a feast) on a Saturday in November. This happened when Mama invited the local butcher, Herr Lulay, to come to our house and slaughter our pig. I was never able to watch when this happened because pigs are very smart. I also loved our pigs because they made always a variety of noises. It always screamed when it was chased out of its stall. I was hiding for a while that I didn't hear or see anything. After the killing part was over, Herr Lulay started sorting the meat. The meat inspector arrived shortly after. He inspected the meat microscopically to make sure that the pig was healthy and its meat was good for consumption. Some meat was being smoked, others cooked. Mama knew a blacksmith who canned the meat for us. This was the best method to prevent it from getting spoiled. Refrigeration and freezing was not available in those days. On that day, we feasted on Sauerkraut, pea puree, and boiled belly-pork. It was yummy. Herr Lulay made tiny liverwurst sausages and sausage soup, which we shared with neighbors.

The interesting part was that the butcher had the same name as my father, Hans Lulay, and he had four daughters, too. We were not related in any way. My mother's sister, Aunt Gretel, and her daughter, Marga, from Ober-Abtsteinach, came to help because Mama would not have managed this alone. My cousin Marga was my age. In Kirschhausen, we had classes on Saturdays every other week. Before my graduation, Marga usually accompanied me to school when the Schlachtfest fell on a Saturday and I had classes.

My mother always kept a sizable chunk of suet on the side for the woodpecker. Every winter, this welcomed guest would come to our shed and loved this big treat for its survival.

1959 Castro becomes dictator of Cuba
Alaska and Hawaii become states

Beside the pig, we always had twelve to fourteen chickens. They were so well-trained that it was amusing to watch their transfer in the morning and evening. They stayed overnight in the henhouse in the shed, and the day was spent in a large, fenced-in chicken scoop. When they left the henhouse, especially in the beginning, all of us had to stay about five feet away from the shed, arms outstretched, to guide the chicken to the daytime chicken scoop. After a while, they had learned the routine, and they would no longer scream and flatter into all directions.

We also needed to protect our chickens from the Gypsies. During the summer time, they travelled with their motor homes throughout Germany and camped in Kirschhausen at the nearby forest at the Weber's Heck. They stopped especially in villages and sold sewing items, mostly yarn. We always had to be concerned and left all the doors locked when they had come to our village. They tried to sell their items, and if you didn't purchase anything, they got quite angry and loud. When the doorbell rang, we had to make sure not to open the door and speak only through a small built in window in the door. At times, they kept on talking and talking to steal your time. In the meantime, while the Gypsy was still at the door and talking, another Gypsy took some eggs from the hen house, or entered another unlocked door where he found cheese or anything worthwhile to take along. We always had to warn neighbors, and they let us know that the Gypsies had returned again. From where they came from, we didn't know. They seemed to be Romani people, which is a nomadic ethnic group. They live mostly in Europe and the Americas and originated in the northern regions of the Indian subcontinent.

I played a lot with Ruth and Ingeborg, the daughters of our butcher. At times, we used the lilac near the Weber's Heck as our meeting spot. The lilac was one of my favorite shrubs because of its scent and warm color. Other white-blooming trees flourished there, too. However, the lilac is strongly in my memory because after the war many songs had been written with soldiers in mind. There is this one verse from a song…

Dreimal blueht er schon der Flieder	Three times the lilac is now blooming
Der Soldat kehrt niemals wieder	The soldier does not return again
In sein Heimatland zurueck	To his homeland
Denn er hat sein junges Leben	Because he gave his young life
Seinem Vaterland gegeben	For his Vaterland
Und geopfert ihm sein Glueck	And sacrificed his own happiness

Now I'm in my seventies and have a lilac in my backyard. Every May when the lilac is blooming, I sing the entire song, especially the above verse because I'm a child of a world war.

ISABELL VON DER WALDESRUH

Once in a while, Agnes and I needed to clean out and organize the drawers in the kitchen cupboard. I remember when Agnes and I found three colored, hand drawn pictures in the form of a postcard. On each postcard was a little girl. One card was addressed to Agnes, one to Irene, and another one to Marianne. I never had received one because I was not born yet when they were created. These postcards Papa sent from Russia to my three older sisters. A fellow soldier drew these cards for him. They were so well done, and I always wished that I would have gotten one, too. Long after my father's death, this close comrade from the war who drew the cards visited my mother on a regular basis. My mother found strength in his visit. She was always reminded of what a wonderful man she had married, but lost too soon.

We four sisters and our mother sang a lot and this brought great harmony to our family. It continued even after my older sisters got married, but it happened less often. Agnes played the Harmonica. Following is a favorite one of mine among many:

Beim Holderstrauch	At the elder brush
Im Holderstrauch, im Holderstrauch	The elder brush, the elder brush
Der bluehte schoen im Mai	so beautifully bloomed in May

Da sang ein kleines Voegelein	There a little bird did sing
Ein Lied von Lieb und Treu	A song of love and loyalty
Beim Holderstrauch, beim Holderstrauch	At the elder brush, the elder brush
Wir sassen Hand in Hand	We were sitting hand in hand
Wir waren in der Maienzeit	In the tides of May we were
Die Gluecklichsten im Land	The Happiest in all the land
Beim Holderstrauch, beim Holderstrauch	At the elder brush, the elder brush
Da musst' geschieden sein	Once parted we did pine
Komm bald zurueck, komm bald zurueck	Come back soon, come back soon
Du allerliebste mein	You dearest love of mine
Beim Holderstrauch, beim Holderstrauch	At the elder brush, the elder brush
Da weint ein Maegd'lein sehr	There a girl so oft did cry

Der Vogel schweigt, der	The bird silenced, the el-
Holderstrauch	der brush
Der blueht schon lang'	Its roots already did dry
nicht mehr	

It is quite difficult to translate the songs into the English language in order to make any sense.

Mama was a pious woman and had a great taste for beauty as well. At the front of our house, right in the middle between two windows, she had a little shrine built into the house with the Blessed Mother and the child Jesus. This little shrine was surrounded with rose vines, and the roses bloomed all summer long. Inside this shrine, she had a red, electric light burning at night. This was my mother's faith. Down in the garden below, where all the vegetables grew, she had planted along the creek inside the fence and throughout the garden the most beautiful peonies and lilies. In the northwest corner of the garden, a white Arabian jasmine garden shrub stood in full bloom all summer long. Its beauty and its scent when you reached the garden door was so impressive that I wished that it would have never stopped flowering.

Coming home from an in-patient stay at Heidelberg during my school years and returning back to classes needed always some kind of adjustment. I enjoyed all kinds of needlework and embroidery while at school. I also was a good student in the other subjects, but Lehrer Nack, My teacher in 4th and 5th grade, was less understanding about my condition. He didn't want to be bothered when my mother needed to talk to him. Despite this, I still liked the way he taught. We had lessons in the afternoon because the room was needed in the morning for the other grades.

Struwwel was still my best friend. I read endless books, mostly those written for girls. I had two favorite stories: *Das doppelte Lottchen (Lottie and Lisa)* and *Der sanfte Falke (The Gentle Hawk)*. My first movie at the movie theatre in Heppenheim was "*Serengeti darf nicht sterben*" or "*Serengeti must not die.*" My entire school attended this movie.

When I was in 5th grade, I received a big doll house for Christmas. It was furnished with a bedroom, livingroom, and kitchen. The window had real curtains. We, I mean my sister, Agnes, and my cousin, Gerda, spent many hours playing with this doll house rearranging the furniture, pretending to cook meals, and dressing and undressing the little dolls, some originated in South Africa.

I remember fully one December 6th, the feast day of St. Nikolaus. I could have been six or seven years old. I don't recall whether my father was still alive. I ambled down my street, the Honerbachstrasse. It was early evening and had just started getting dark. I peeked into all directions whether St. Nikolaus and Knecht Ruprecht, his helper, who usually wore a long, grey coat, a big, black hat, had a scrubby beard, carried a chain and a sack for the goodies, walked already the streets. When I was at the beginning of the Honerbachstrasse and had reached the Heppenheimerstrasse, I heard the rattling of chains. I became so frightened. I took the curve back to the Honerbachstrasse and then lost both of my slippers. It was quite cold. I raced back home, but my feet hurt from all the little pebbles and sand. Shortly after, they both arrived at our house. I was still shaking because I knew that when children didn't behave, they would get punished by Knecht Ruprecht. I was instructed by St. Nikolaus, he was dressed as bishop, to say the Our Father… I then prayed the Our Father and was very respectful toward St. Nikolaus and Knecht Ruprecht. I responded with yes and no to all the questions of St. Nikolaus. When he started speaking with me, I got even more nervous, but his conversation with me was not frightening. He handed me apples and various nuts. I then realized that he was pleased with me. Only good children would get fruit and nuts.

Between Christmas and New Year, Mama was baking pretzels for New Year's Day. During my childhood,

I visited on New Year's Day our neighbor down the street, the Umhauer family. They lived at the very end of the Honerbachstrasse. I stood in an upright position in front of their closed door and said the medieval lyric poem in the local dialect:

Ich winsch Eich	I wish you
A glickliches neies Yoar	A happy New Year
Gsundheit, longes Laewe	Health, a long life
Friede un Glickseligkeit	Peace and happiness
Ewisch Glick, Seligkeit	Good fortune, bliss
Amen! Bauf!	Amen! Bauf!

When I said "Amen! Bauf!" I punched the door with my fist and gave it a hard blow. After that, they opened the door with gracious expressions on their faces and handed me a pretzel and a present. I loved going there every New Year's Day.

As spring was close at hand, Mama had signed up for a bus trip to Trier, which our parish community had arranged. It was a pleasantly warm day. She had decided to take me along. I was the only child among the adult women. Trier is a city on the banks of the Moselle. It lies in a valley between low vine-covered hills of red sandstone in the west of the state of Rhineland-Palatinate, near the border with Luxembourg. It has a rich history, but we visited only The Porta Nigra and the Cathedral of Trier. The Porta Nigra was founded by the Romans, and it contains several well-preserved Roman structures like the Porta Nigra gate. At the cathedral, we visited the *Heilige Rock (Holy Robe)*. It is a relic which is preserved at the Cathedral of Trier. It is supposed to contain fragments of the shroud of Jesus Christ. The legend according to the Gospel of St. John, the shroud of Jesus after the crucifixion had been divided into four pieces and raffled off amongst the soldiers. The undergarment, however, was not divided, but allotted to one soldier because it was woven throughout without a seam. According to tradition, St. Helena, the mother of Constantine the Great, brought the Holy Shroud to Trier.

As a child, we travelled by foot every year with other faith filled people to the St. Walburga chapel, which was located in the middle of the forest and in walking distance from Kirschhausen. To this day, there are annual pilgrimages. St. Walburga lived from 710 – 779. She was one of the most popular saints of the Middle Ages. She was born and educated by English Benedictines. St. Boniface asked England for help in the missionary work in Germany. St. Walburga was open to this call. She left her homeland in England and devoted her life to the conversion of Germany. St. Walburga became the Abbess of a double Benedictine Monastery in Heidenheim. She was responsible for the spiritual and material welfare of both the monks and the nuns…

The Light Miracle, one of many, is attributed to her. One night when Walburga asked one of the monks to light the candles so she could go to her room, he refused. Walburga had to find her way alone in the dark. When her sisters came to accompany her to supper, the hallway was lighted not by candles, but by a divine light. It lit the dormitory brightly until time for the office of Matins. The nuns went to Walburga, filled with joy over the miracle, and she prayed to the Lord in these words: **"Oh Lord, as a humble maid who committed my life to you since my youth, I thank you for granting this grace. You have honored me in my unworthiness with the comfort of your light. This sign gives courage to the souls of your handmaids who are dependent on me. And you have driven out the darkness and our fear through the bright light of your mercy."** St. Walburga is buried in Eichstaett, Germany.

For one thousand years, mysterious moisture has collected every year on St. Walburga's relics. This water became known as "St. Walburga's Oil", and was seen as a sign of her continuing intercession. The oil has always been collected and given to pilgrims. Healings, attributed to St. Walburga's intercession, continue to be reported up to the present day. I feel blessed to have three vials of "St. Walburga Oil" in my refrigerator.

On Saturday, December 26, 1959, my sister, Irene, married Peter Kohl from Ober-Abtsteinach, which also used to be Mama's hometown. Our grandmother was still alive and aunts, uncles, and cousins still lived there. It was a nice little village surrounded by hills and mountains. But Irene missed Kirschhausen and the home she came from. On those weekends when they didn't come for a visit to Kirschhausen, she wanted me to be with her in Ober-Abtsteinach. I always had the feeling that her marriage was an unhappy one. They had three children. She never complained. She visited me twice in Highlands Ranch, Colorado, the first time with her husband, Peter, and the second time with her Son, Alexander and the boy, Kevin. She would have loved to visit me again, but she got ill with breast cancer. Shortly before she passed on, her son, Richard, and daughter-in-law, Nicole, positioned her on Skype, and I had a chance to talk with her for the last time. She didn't say anything, she just looked at me. I strongly believe that she recognized me, but I saw in her face the death sentence. She waved good-bye. She knew. My sister, Irene, passed away in the hospital in Heppenheim on July 23, 2010.

1960 Lasers invented
U-2 spy plane shot down over Soviet Union

During the 1960s, petticoats and ponytails had become the latest fashion, but the petticoats scratched on my legs and the nylons got ripped in no time. I loved my ponytail and later on bundled it up on top of my head. My friend, Christel, started working right after she got out of school. It was important to her to earn money right away. Soon after, she had saved enough money and chose to visit Austria. She wrote me a card from there and on the bottom it read, Liebe Gruesse, Christel und Gerhard (Greetings, Christel and Gerhard). I dreaded this day. I wished that this would never have happened. She had a boyfriend now, and I was alone again. I don't remember whether I was jealous or envious, but I felt sorry for myself. A few years later, Christel got married to Gerhard. She had a big wedding because both sides had many family members. They celebrated at home, as it used to be in those days. I stopped by with a present and wished them all the best in their marriage. I was offered to eat some pie with coffee and chose gooseberry pie, my favorite. It was yummy.

My friend, Christel, and I

When I turned 16, I was allowed to go with Christel to the parish fair dancing, but only in the afternoon. Later on, I got the permission to go in the evening as well. My health was very important to me. I learned early in life to be disciplined enough not to drink any alcoholic beverages, and I left the dance party early that I did get plenty of sleep. Alcohol and medication don't agree with one another. I stayed that way when I started dating. To this day, I still follow the same conviction. When I was a child and there was carnival in Kirschhausen, I saved the money I had collected from relatives until the very end. I seldom took a ride. One time, I purchased for two Deutsche Mark a white, long-haired dog. I kept this dog for a long time in the oak cabinet in our living-room. My cousin, Marga, invited me from time to time to attend dance parties in Ober-Abtsteinach. This was a good opportunity for Mama to drive with me to her childhood home and village. After Irene and Peter had gotten married, I went dancing with them as well.

Sometimes I went with Brigitte, another friend from Kirschhausen, to Sonderbach to listen to Franz Lambert playing on the organ. He is a famous German composer, organist, and an avid Hammond organ player. Sonderbach is in walking distance from Kirschhausen. Franz and I grew up together because the people from Sonderbach attended the church in Kirschhausen. During his career, he released over 100 albums. What I like about him is that he remained the same as he used to be when we were growing up.

My sister, Irene, had arranged a job for me through the staff department head, Herrn Gloetzke. I was excited and drove with my mother by bus to Heppenheim to purchase some new dresses. I liked my new job, took dictations, and had many other duties. My boss, Herr Hilse, was from Berlin. When he talked very fast, I had a hard time to follow him because of his Berlinerisch (Berlin dialect). I served him tea at 9:00 a.m. He then said, "Danke, mein Kindchen!" ("Thank you, my little child!") My co-worker, Fraeulein Fischer, was from Dresden, and she wore expensive jewelry. Herr Hilse and Fraeulein Fischer had been bombed out and arrived in Weinheim after the war. My condition was stable. I liked the work, but it was not easy for me to catch the bus at 6:15 a.m. to Heppenheim and then take the train to Weinheim. I had to walk for about 15 - 20 minutes from the train station to the department Metalastik, where I worked. The evening was a repeat of the morning, except the other way around. While working there, I took the opportunity to take English courses, which the company offered free of charge. I enjoyed this very much, and my teacher told me that I should spend some time in England because I was doing so well. I studied the vocabulary while riding the train and when sitting at the station concourse in Heppenheim waiting for the bus to Kirschhausen.

1961   Berlin Wall
         USSR puts first human in space

13 August 1961 was a sad day in German history. German communists closed the border between Soviet-controlled East Berlin and democratic controlled western section of the city. Refugees were stopped from leaving in order to flee to West Germany. In August, Soviet Premier Minister Nikita Khrushchev gave the go ahead to the Communist leader of East Germany, Walter Ulbricht, to seal off all access between East and West Berlin. During August 12 – 13, soldiers began overnight laying more than 100 miles of barbed wire. The wire was replaced by a six-foot-high, 96 mile-long wall of concrete blocks. For added security they placed guard towers, machine gun posts, and searchlights on the wall with patrols day and night. Many tried to escape. Some were successful, others failed. Then they raised the wall to 10 feet high.

In 1961, the German movie "Soweit die Fuesse tragen" (As far as my feet will carry me) aired. Every Sunday, I followed it at the Villa Rosemary on their guest television.

A German World War II prisoner of war, Clemens Forell, escapes from a Siberian Gulag in the Soviet Union back to Germany. Later on, I also purchased the book. The plot involved Clemens Forell, a German soldier, who was captured by the Soviets in 1945. I always thought the same could have happened to my father after the war.

Forell was sentenced to 25 years hard labor for "crimes against the partisans" and sent with others to a far northeastern labor camp in the Soviet Union. When they arrived at the gulag, they were already half dead because of starvation rations. After one unsuccessful attempt, Forell escaped with the assistance of Dr. Stauffer, the camp doctor. Dr. Stauffer was terminally ill with cancer, and he no longer had the desire to escape. He gave Forell warm clothes and a loaded pistol. He also explained to him where he could find hidden supplies. He wandered across northern Siberia, killed seals for food, until he met two gold prospectors, Semyon and Anastas. Conflicts arose between these three and a suspicious Semyon threw Forell down a slope. Surrounded by wolves, Forell was rescued by nomadic Chukchi herders, one of whom, named Irina, fell in love with him. Forell made a full recovery, but the Chukchi learned that the Soviets were looking for Forell. Much to Irina's heartache, Forell left. The Chukchi gave him their dog as a companion. He ran into a logging operation and was sent on the train with the freight as a brakeman. Through betrayal, he was again nearly captured by the Soviets with Kamenev as its leader. Forell managed to escape, but his dog was shot and killed when he attacked Kamenev, leaving him severely scarred. Forell advanced to Central Asia. A Polish Jewish man helped him acquire a passport, despite the fact that Forell was German. Forell traveled to the Iranian border. As he assumed that his way is toward freedom, he noticed Kamenev walking toward him from the Iranian side. They stared at each other. Strangely enough, Kamenev stepped aside and let Forell pass, proclaiming "the victory is mine". Once on the Iranian side, Forell was taken prisoner, believed to be a Soviet spy. However, his uncle who worked in Ankara, Turkey, was brought in to identify him. Forell received his freedom and arrived in Germany at Christmas. While he saw his family leaving for church, he immediately walked to the church where he was reunited with his loved ones.

This movie captured me so much that I looked forward to Sunday afternoons. I learned some Russian words at the same time, like "Dawai, Dawai", which has several meanings and in the movie meant "Go on, go on".

After working in Weinheim for 1 ½ years, I decided to investigate whether I could find similar work closer to Kirschhausen. Then I learned about an opening at the German government in Heppenheim for the non-cash payment transactions. I applied, got the job, and liked it a lot. I was able to sleep longer in the morning. Before work started, I attended Mass at St. Peter's Basilica in Heppenheim, which was located right next to my place of work. In the evening, I arrived back home before dark. I found more time for myself. One morning when I arrived at work, my co-worker, Frau Daniel, had called in ill. She was in charge of the payroll. I was instructed to do her work the following day. This was quite troubling to me because this was beyond my training and experience. I knew that I couldn't do it. The next morning when I walked to the bus station I collapsed right there. Whether it was a seizure or not, I do not know, but most likely it was. Then I spent six months at the University Clinic in Heidelberg. The psychological part was also a reason I had to stay so long. However, I was allowed to go out, go to the movies, or go shopping. At one time, I met a girl from Hamburg, Charlotte Singer. She was very nice and we became friends. She was found in a hotel in Heidelberg and had tried to commit suicide by cutting open her wrist. There was quite a difference between the two of us. She was a city girl, and I was more a country girl. She invited me to come to Hamburg, but it never happened. I wanted to give her a present so she would feel that she was loved. She didn't tell me why she was tired of living. I drew a horse on the wrong side of white fake leather. Cut out two pieces and a middle piece to give that horse a body. I started stitching the body with the outside pieces together, filled it with cotton, and then finished it up. I don't remember what made me choose a white horse. Was it symbolism or mythology? She loved that horse and appreciated it a lot.

When you have seizures, you must go through a lot because the world around you doesn't understand you. It seemed that way to me. When I was discharged, I was afraid to return to my job. I was hoping I could work at the clinic as an occupational therapist because I was able to create exceptional things and assist other patients. Out of cork, I carved the most beautiful train with locomotive and four wagons, or fashioned a doll with long hair. With that hair I created a tight bun on top of her head. I embroidered her eyes, nose, and lips that she looked real and clothed her with a red-checkered dress. The sleeves had white ruffles at the front. However, I didn't want to leave my mother alone because my two other sisters had also gotten married. So I decided to return to my workplace at the German government, but somehow I didn't feel comfortable anymore. My treating physician at the clinic encouraged me not to return to that place. Also, when I returned for work, the main boss made some nasty comments. I left that place even though I didn't have another job lined up yet. In order to pay for my health insurance, I made moccasins for a gentleman in Sonderbach who distributed them. It was a relaxing job and I loved working with my hands, but the pay was not enough to live on. While I was a patient at the clinic in Heidelberg, I stayed in contact with my primary care physician in Heppenheim.

1962 Cuban Missile Crisis

There was another girl friend of mine who lived next to Christel. Her name was Brigitte with whom I went occasionally to Sonderbach to listen to Franz Lambert. She became manic-depressive when she turned fourteen and went on a weight-loss diet. During her healthy time, she was a great friend, but we didn't get to see each other often because she attended a different school in another city. After my father had died, I always told her that I was adopted. Her family was rich and owned the quarry and employed many people. I'm still puzzled to this day why I felt that way and told her that I was adopted. My family was not as wealthy as her family, but this didn't matter. When her brother was ordained a priest, she walked down the street with her boyfriend and called out, "This is nothing for two people who are deeply in love!" I always doubted that her illness was caused by a reducing diet. She got married and later divorced. When I got married, she stood outside the church and waited for me. She knew that I would be leaving for the United States soon. In 1976, when I already lived in the United States and visited my family in Germany, I met her mother and learned from her that Brigitte had started writing a letter to me, but didn't finish it; instead she committed suicide. It had just happened when I arrived in Germany. I was able to attend her funeral. Her brother was the presiding priest. What I felt, I just cannot describe. Almost all former classmates attended Brigitte's funeral. It was nice to meet so many, but the circumstances were indeed sad ones.

The local priest, Pfarrer Wolf, was trembling while writing. He had asked me whether I could write for him the parish register transcripts. While accepting this honor, I was able to read about my father's death. It was written in such a comforting way that it gave me peace, and I was able to arrive at some kind of closure about my father's death.

Throughout the year, there were quite a few religious feast days in Kirschhausen with processions through the streets. Some took up to two hours. We prayed and sang for good weather and protection for the crops while walking through the fields. Corpus Christi was a solemn feast day with procession up and down the Heppenheimerstrasse. The streets were decorated with chopped off life trees and the windows of the houses with candles, Christian figurines, crucifixes, and sacred linens. The priest stopped on three altars for prayer and benediction. First communicants walked directly in front of the priest who carried the Holy Eucharist. The children in their First Communion attire strewed rose petals on the ground, and the church choir with trumpets shared in the festivities.

Growing up without a father or brother was extremely difficult for me when I was dating and later on in my marriage. I had some father figures in my life like my physicians in Heidelberg. I took them on as father figures. Later on, my boss, Dr. Berg, was an awesome man. He invited me to their family parties, especially when his daughters had something to celebrate. My brother-in-laws affected me on a different level. They belonged to my sisters. We played a lot of card games and other games, but I didn't feel any security.

1963   JFK assassinated
         Profumo scandal in UK

When I had returned home again from my stay in Heidelberg, it happened that Dr. Berg lost his medical assistant. He saw my mother from time to time because German doctors still made home visits. Mama probably had shared with him that I'm not happy anymore, and that my doctor at the clinic in Heidelberg had told me to leave the government job. Dr. Berg told my mother, "I would love to take Rita!" I was thrilled to hear that. I immediately called Dr. Berg. We had a wonderful conversation and I started working the next day. For the start, we decided for only half a day. I loved every minute of it. After a brief time, I felt well enough to work full time. He was happy with my work. After working for him for three months, he entrusted me with the tasks of giving injections, doing lab work, and the usage of all the medical equipment that he kept in his office for treating his patients. I signed up for evening courses, dissected a frog, and studied other interesting things about the blood. Dr. Berg invited me to have lunch with the family at noon and tea at mid-afternoon. I accepted this invitation. His wife cooked mainly Eastern European fare. She was a native of Romania. Mama had never made stuffed peppers, but they were quite often on the menu at Dr. Berg's, and the peppers were covered with sweet cream. Not to disappoint anyone at the table, I ate the peppers, but I got up right afterwards, ran to the bathroom, and they got out much quicker than I ate them.

1964

Patients at Dr. Berg's office preferred that I should give them their prescribed injections intravenously, subcutaneous, and intramuscular. Dr. Berg had no problems with that. He also took me along to a nearby international school to assist him when the students got their annual Flu shots. I loved my job and was quite happy. It affected also my general health by feeling respected and appreciated. I have stayed in contact with my co-worker, Anke, from many years ago via Facebook. Wednesday afternoons, the office was closed. Dr. Berg's youngest daughter, Karin, loved to come with me to Kirschhausen and spend the afternoon with me at our house.

1965   U.S. sends troops to Vietnam
        Watts riots in Los Angeles

In 1965, I joined a youth group on a trip to Berlin. It was an unbelievable shock to see my country divided by a wall, barbed wire, and mines. I was aware of it, but you have to see it in order to believe this brutality. A memorial in the form of a cross was erected for those who attempted to flee but perished during this undertaking. The east side of the wall looked abandoned, almost like a ghost town. The houses had no glass in the windows, and the VoPo (German People's Police) sat in the windows staring at the west. At the Checkpoint-Charlie, the sign read: SIE VERLASSEN DEN AMERIKANISCHEN SEKTOR – YOU ARE LEAVING THE AMERICAN SECTOR.

We continued on and visited the Olympic Stadium. In 1936, Jesse Owens from the United States won four gold medals: 100 meters, 200 meters, long jump, and 4 x 100 relay. At the Memorial Ploetzensee, we held a quiet moment in honor of the more than 3,000 people from inside and outside Germany who were wrongly executed under the National Socialism Regime. Then we drove to the Berlin Zoo, the Wannsee, to Grunewald for a more relaxing fare. The following day, I took pictures of the *Seelenbohrer.* The people of Berlin gave this name to the bell tower of the Kaiser-Friedrich-Gedaechtnis-Kirche. We passed the Reichtagsgebaeude and visited the Kongresshalle (Congress Hall). Again, they have their own name for this building. They call the Kongresshalle *Schwangere Auster* (pregnant oyster). The visit to Berlin was quite an emotional trip, but I had many wonderful experiences, especially with the other participants on this trip.

My two cousins, both named Gerda, Rudi Luschtinetz, and some other friends drove on a hot summer day to Heidelberg and rented a boat and paddled up and down the Neckar River. We all had a great time, especially since Heidelberg had become a second home to me.

1966   Chinese Cultural Revolution begins

In 1966, Mama needed hospitalization at the women's clinic in Darmstadt because she was diagnosed with cancer. I visited her on Sunday, but the previous evening, I attended with Gerda Roemer a dance party in Fuerth/Odenwald. I met Klaus Peter Malsch and he asked me for a dance. He became my future husband. He wanted to meet me the next day, but I told him that I needed to go to Darmstadt in the afternoon to the women's clinic. To this day, I recall the question he had asked me, "Are you a nurse?" I said, "No, I'm going to visit my mother." From that point on we met regularly. He didn't own a car at that time because buses and trains used to be a good and dependable transportation. As we got to know each other better, I helped him financially getting a car. As soon as he became a proud owner, we went every Sunday on excursions and dined at restaurants which were known to serve good food but not too pricey. On Easter Sunday, March 26, 1967, we got engaged. Celebrating with us at our house were his parents, Mama, my three sisters with husbands, and nieces and nephews. Our living-room was so nicely decorated with candles and flowers. We used Mama's best dishes and silverware. I wore a lilac dress, which I had purchased in Weinheim. Marianne baked and decorated a Black-Forest-Cherry Torte and Irene made her famous Butter Cream Torte.

During my stay at Dr. Berg's, I had inquired about spending some time at a health spa. I informed Dr. Berg that I would like to use my vacation for that. I vacationed for four weeks in beautiful Bad Hermannsborn near Bad Driburg, North Rhine-Westphalia, also close to Bielefeld. I received peat packs. These changed the color of my hair to red-brown and the handles of my purse to red. I shared a huge and elegant room with two other girls. One day, we drove together with three other gentlemen to Bad Pyrmont. It is a town in the district of Hamelin-Pyrmont, in Lower Saxony, Germany, and is located on the River Emmer, about 10 km west of the Weser. Bad Pyrmont is a popular spa resort that gained its reputation as a fashionable place for princely vacations in the 17 and 18th centuries. The six of us visited the Award Winning Park and took quite a few pictures. It was also a fun day, and our physician in Bad Hermannsborn had given us the permission to visit Bad Pyrmont. One of the girls was also a Medical Assistant as myself and came from Halle on the river Saale. It reminded me always of the song "An der Saale hellem Strande..." ("At the fair banks of the Saale...") Mama wrote me a letter to Bad Hermannsborn. I treasure this letter very much and keep it in a special file.

1967   Canada's Centennial
Six-Day War
Summer of Love

During the summer of 1967, Klaus Peter and I vacationed in Austria. We stayed in St. Gilgen at Lake Wolfgang and took the cable car up to the Alpine pasture where we met a beautiful St. Bernard dog. At one of the huts, they offered us some hardy bread and Alpine cheese with fresh milk from Alpine cows. From there we boarded another cable car which brought us up to the Zwoelferhorn. Its height is 4,993 feet. The view of St. Gilgen and Lake Wolfgang was spectacular. The next day we continued on to Salzburg and visited the Mirabellengarten. We toured the Dachsteingebirge, a mountain chain of the Alps. But after a while I informed Klaus Peter that I wanted to go home earlier than planned because Mama was hospitalized. I had three other sisters to look after her, but somehow I was drawn to go home to be with her. Also, Klaus Peter got called by Siemens, the company he worked for, to transfer to Erlangen for a while to work at the German headquarter. He accepted the offer and moved to Erlangen after our return from vacation, and he was only able to drive home every other week. Instead of him coming home every other week, I took the train and visited him in Erlangen. At one time, I stayed for the Erlanger Bergkirchweih, an annual Volksfest or beer festival and travelling funfair, which starts on the Thursday before Pentecost. This carnival draws about one million people from English-speaking countries. The food and festivities can be compared to the Octoberfest in Munich. But something did not agree with me in Erlangen and I needed to take charcoal tablets.

In the evening, after leaving Dr. Berg's office at 5:30 p.m., I drove from Heppenheim to Kirschhausen by bus. It stopped right in front of Marianne's house in Kirschhausen. From time to time, I visited her briefly and chatted with my three nieces and four nephews. Marianne's family had grown rather quickly. It bothered my mother that I stopped by at Marianne's house before coming home. I think that she was lonely. Her health was declining as well.

In the fall of 1967, Klaus Peter and I travelled by car to Passau, also called the City of the Three Rivers. The river Danube meets the Inn and the Ilz. This proud and picturesque city lies in the far southeast corner near the Austrian border. I loved their cobblestone streets like those in Heppenheim. They are not for high heel shoes. The Old Town created by Italian baroque masters in the 17th century shows soaring towers, picturesque places, promenades, and romantic lanes. In the heart of Passau rises St. Stephen's Cathedral, in which the world's largest cathedral organ sounds. In St. Stephen's Cathedral we enjoyed a breathtaking concert. High above the rivers, the majestic fortress Veste Oberhaus on the Danube's side and the Pilgrimage Church "Maria Hilf" on the Inn's side display an outstanding beauty. I found Passau the most spectacular city on the Danube.

Peter had been asked by his employer whether he would like to work for three years in the United States. He didn't give an answer right away because he wanted to discuss this with me first. When he approached me with this, I was shocked because I did not know what answer to give him. He said that he will not accept the offer if I don't go with him. I was torn apart. We were engaged, but I lived at home with my very ill mother. After thinking this over, I decided to go with him. It meant also giving up my job at Dr. Berg's medical office. These were not easy decisions, but somehow I weighed it out and told him that I will go with him. This also indicated getting married a little sooner than planned.

I must say that I was not particularly fond of Dr. Berg's wife who was a physician, too. At one time she said to me, "We only took you in that you don't get lost." This was another slap in the face because I had no degree or any papers of a specific education. It hurt. But I knew that my journey was not an ordinary one. There was not much I could have done differently. Life can be very difficult and merciless. I'm sure that Dr. Berg didn't know what she had revealed to me. Both went their own ways. Was she jealous of me? I knew I was appreciated by my boss.

In November of 1967 Mama was not feeling well at all. She had lost a lot of weight, her cheeks had become bony, and she was yellow-pale all the time. Dr. Berg referred her to the hospital in Heppenheim. At the hospital, she asked me what she should do with the house. Did she sense that she was going to die? I immediately answered, "Do whatever you want. We are going now." I think I was a little rude to her. Dr. Stockhammer, her treating physician, would not tell us anything. We sisters decided to take her home for Christmas and not return her to the hospital. Klaus Peter and I made marriage preparations and attended for three consecutive Sundays seminars in Weinheim in order to learn all about the responsibilities of a Christian marriage. We also needed to make plans what to take along to the United States. I typed out a list of every single item that I thought would be important. An extremely difficult part was to let Dr. Berg know that I would be leaving him.

We visited Gerda and Mac in Kaiserslautern. We also took her mother along. Klaus Peter and I had many questions about life in America. Her husband, a GI, was stationed with the military in Kaiserslautern, Germany.

1968   Martin Luther King assassinated
RFK assassinated
Tet Offensive in Vietnam
Prague Spring

When I informed Dr. Berg that I'm leaving with my future husband for the United States, he was upset. Remembering what his wife said to me, I also said that it doesn't make sense to work here anymore. I don't know whether he understood. I should have told him. However, this would not have changed anything. We always visited them after we had moved to the United States and vacationed in Germany. I stayed in contact with him until he passed away.

Klaus Peter and I got married

February came along and we got married by the mayor of Kirschhausen, Heinrich Schaefer, on Friday, the 23rd, when we took our vows before the world. On Sunday, February 25th, 1968, we got married in the St. Bartholomaeuskirche (Church of St. Bartholomew) in Kirschhausen. We took our vows before God. Mama was unable to attend. Klaus Peter arranged for special speakers and placed it in her room next to her bed that she could hear the entire church ceremony. However, something went wrong and there was no connection. We celebrated afterwards at Villa Rosemary, just my sisters with their husbands and their children and Klaus Peter's parents. I also had invited my Godmother. Klaus Peter's cousin, Wolfgang with his wife Christa, made a surprise visit, coming from Hohenstein/Taunus, which is a mountain range in Hesse, Germany, north of Frankfurt. While celebrating at Villa Rosemary, I walked to the house to Mama several times, just to include her in my special day. I wore a beautiful white wedding gown that I had purchased with my sister, Irene, in Mannheim. Afterwards, Mama's condition went downhill. Her brothers and sisters arrived and wanted to see her. She said "Good bye" to everyone present. Without any second thoughts, I said, "Papa is waiting for you!" Irene got on me harshly, "How can you say something like that. She doesn't know that she is dying!" However, I had the feeling that this was comforting her. After a while she said to me, "Rita, don't forget your faith when you go to America!" I just answered, "Oh no!" I took turns with Marianne to look after Mama. I cared for her children while she stayed with Mama. Irene lived in Ober Abtsteinach, and Agnes with family lived downstairs in our house. Mama died on Wednesday, February 28, 1968, three days after my wedding. 1968 was also a leap year. Dr. Berg was on vacation when I got married. He wouldn't send me a card or anything. He was upset that I left him. His mother, Frau Dr. Berg, senior, handed me a large and quite colorful bouquet of flowers. I had a good relationship with Dr. Berg's mother. Wednesday mornings, it was always her, Anke, and I, when Dr. Berg made house visits in Hambach.

Newly married was supposed to be a joyful time but it was for me a painful time. My mother was gone. My three older sisters wanted to see her one more time before she got buried and went to the chapel at the cemetery. It was not common in Germany at that time to refresh the body, so my mother had changed dramatically after being deceased for hours. I wanted to keep her in memory as she looked when she was alive and healthy. I did the right thing.

April 19, 1968, had arrived and it was the time to leave for the United States. Before my departure, the communication between the four of us was estranged. Irene said to me, "You have no profession." Here I go again, I thought. I think one of my sisters said, "Don't you know that you are ill?" I was doing fine when it came to my health. Klaus Peter and I would not have gone to the United States.

Dr. Berg wouldn't give me the small pox immunization, which was still required at that time. So I went to the health department, and I had no reactions in any way. The absence seizures had been controlled for some years. My belief was that three years are not a long time and when that time is over that we will return to Germany again. All three sisters came to the Frankfurt International Airport. Marianne had this initiated and encouraged my two other sisters by saying to them, "We might never see her again!" This was good, so we were able to be sisters again and saying Good bye to each other, even though our mother was gone. We were all married, and Marianne, Irene, and Agnes had started a family. It was my first flight ever, and I was extremely thirsty and drank orange juice from Frankfurt to Chicago.

When we arrived in Chicago, there was nobody there to pick us up as we were told. Not used to seeing colored people in Germany, I saw not far from us a heavy-set, colored man. He was sitting on his suitcase. I got scared. After a while, Lutz Bock arrived, the gentleman who was designated to pick us up. He drove us to a motel. This was also a new experience, but when you are young, everything is much easier to handle. In the evening, we were invited by Mr. and Mrs. Hausner for dinner at a restaurant. Mr. Hausner was Klaus Peter's American boss for the Chicago area. I wore a sky blue, short-sleeve sweater and on top the matching long-sleeve sweater.

After the first impression of being in the United States, the following day we tried to search for an apartment. It needed to be furnished since our stay in the Chicago area was only for six months. We went to a Real Estate agency, but the problem was the language. The Real Estate people knew Heinz and Helga Hitzemann, a couple from Germany. Through them we communicated with the Real Estate lady. They also assisted us in finding an apartment. They had an adopted daughter. We found a fairly nice and furnished apartment with a large living-room, bedroom, dining-room with kitchen, which had a gas stove, and a full bath was across from the living-room. I had no experience with gas, but I handled it very well. Friedhelm Boeckman, a co-worker to Klaus Peter, lived in Addison. He was so generous and furnished us with a television. This came in handy and was of tremendous help to me improving my English, and I had some entertainment during the day when Klaus Peter was at work. I was not used to commercials and always wondered why this constant interruption and then the continuation of the movie.

One day, I wanted to take a bath instead of a shower. When I turned on the water, out of the plughole flew ants all over the tub. I had never experienced this before. It could have been termites. My first thought was to stop them, and the only thing that entered my mind was using my hairspray. Sure enough, the hairspray worked, but the tub was filled with big flies. Well, we knew that we would not stay in Illinois for long, so we kept the apartment. We visited Zayre, a big discount store in Addison, not far from where we lived. On weekends, we made excursions to Lake Michigan. Since we both came from a hilly landscape, water was quite a refreshing experience. We visited Maria Armtzen who was also from Fuerth, Germany, Klaus Peter's hometown. She initially had purchased Klaus Peter's baby carriage for her child. While we visited her, she was sewing her daughter Waltraud's wedding dress, which she decorated with a lot of pearls. She also shared with us that one of her sons was shot and killed right in front of their house. The Arntzens owned a house at Lake Geneva in Wisconsin, to where she invited us for an afternoon. It was quite a ride. We enjoyed that intimate summer house, the quietness, and the lake's surroundings of pink blooming trees. Klaus Peter and Maria shared stories from their hometown. Since Maria lived in Chicago and we lived in Addison, we didn't get to see each other often. We exchanged Christmas cards every year. This year's card failed to appear.

Then came the day when our car with all our goods arrived from Germany, and we had to go to the port of arrival. In the meantime, we learned that my sister, Agnes, had added potatoes and onions to our items, which we didn't know. We were scared that this could bring us in big trouble. You cannot import food items, especially onions and potatoes. She said that she was concerned that we would have nothing to eat on our arrival in the United States. She is so smart, but this behavior I didn't understand. One co-worker of Klaus Peter went with us in case of emerging problems. Thank God, everything went smoothly, but the potatoes and onions had grown long roots.

The six months in Addison, Illinois, went by so fast. I was busy learning English and studied from the book I had purchased long time ago in Germany for my evening classes. I invited the Hitzeman Family for dinner for helping us with the apartment. The Boeckman Family didn't live far from us, and we spent some afternoons with them and learned about life in America. Frau Boeckman told me, "If you don't belong to a church, nobody is going to bury you." Well, I thought I don't think about dying. I was 24 years old and had the life before me. I was doing well, but I needed to stay on medication.

I realized that I need to find a neurologist who prescribes me the American equivalency of my German medication. When I think back, I was quite courageous. My English was still lousy, and when I called the Mertz Pharmacy in Chicago, nobody would understand me.

The time had come to leave Illinois behind and get on the road to Georgia. It was the end of October 1968. I typed out a letter to our landlord, "We move out!" That took care of it.

We didn't know what to expect in Georgia. We had the address of the Siemens office in Atlanta, Georgia. It was located on Peachtree Street. On our drive to Georgia, we stopped at a dripstone cave, which was lit with colorful lights. Upon arrival in Atlanta, we first went to the Siemens office and met the secretary, Mrs. Eplin. She was a very nice woman, used a lot of make-up and lipstick on her face, black hair, which was probably not her real color, but she was wonderful. I liked her a lot. I was right with my first impression.

We decided to live outside the city and look for a house more south. Wolfgang Ding, a salesman for Siemens, lived in Jonesboro. We went to the local Real Estate lady. She introduced us to Christel Lawson, a German lady from Berlin, to her husband, Bob, an attorney, and to their son, Robby. Christel knew the local builder very well and drove with us to Mr. Kreismennes. He was from Eastern Europe. He showed us houses in progress. We liked one very much, ranch style, three bedrooms, living-room, dining-room, large kitchen, one full bath, and the master bedroom had a bathroom. The house had a two-car garage and at least one acre of land. An olive-green washer and refrigerator stood in the large kitchen. An olive-green dryer was located in the garage. Olive-green was in fashion at that time. I liked the color. A down payment of $900.00 was the only requirement. The cost of the entire house was $16,000.00. We purchased the house and were promised to move in before Christmas.

Christel Lawson offered us to stay with them until we were able to move in. We took that offer. We felt like kings, excited, newly married, and soon to be proud home owners. During the time we stayed with the Lawson family, we visited the Stone Mountain Park in Stone Mountain near Atlanta, Georgia, on a weekend. Wolfgang Ding lived with his wife, Christel, on Flicker Road, which was in walking distance from our new house. Our house was assigned the address 10537 Sandpiper Road. Four other German women lived in Bonanza, which our subdivision in Jonesboro was called.

December came around. We still didn't know for sure whether we would be in the house by Christmas. We kept on hoping. The good news arrived via phone to Christel Lawson just a few days before Christmas. "The house is ready." We hurried out to purchase a Christmas tree. The new house was our present for one another. Winter was basically unknown in Georgia, by far not the way we knew it from Germany.

As soon as Klaus Peter started working, he had to travel a lot by car. He took me along on his trips. We went to various doctor's offices in South Georgia, Valdosta, Norcross, Marietta, hospitals in Atlanta, and I got to know the Georgia landscape. It was also a big culture shock coming from Germany. The people were more laid back, quite friendly, but everything was so different.

1969 First moon landing

There was a small Catholic Mission Church, but I had to find myself where I was when it came to my faith. It took me a while to sort this out. Thoughts and ideas were spinning around in my head, and I got the feeling maybe I was brain washed in Germany in relation to my Catholic faith. I needed to stay away. My next door neighbor, Joyce, took me sometimes to a church. I did not know what to think of it. The behavior of the people was strange. I missed the light which is burning in Catholic churches. This informs you of the presence of Christ in the Holy Eucharist. I didn't see it anywhere. It felt like being just in a room like any other with a group of people who act a little strange. There was nothing spiritual. It is difficult to explain how I felt. Joyce had good intentions, and I'm sure that she was searching.

I didn't have a car or a driver's license. Klaus Peter had a company car. What I liked about Georgia was the Pecans, the moss hanging from the trees, the flowering azalea shrubs, and the Georgia peaches with its many peach trees. I adjusted slowly to their way of life and tried to make the best out of it. In the meantime, I had found a neurologist in Atlanta who changed my medication around to an American brand. I adjusted well to the new medication.

Klaus Peter being an amateur radio operator or ham operator was searching out other hams. Our circle of friends increased. We were invited to parties and the following years to Christmas parties. Soon we became close friends with R. A. and Jessie Carden, an elderly couple. They lived in Hapeville, Georgia.

I started drawing portraits of famous people with charcoal. Soon after, I was introduced to Topper. She owned a studio for ceramics not far from my house on Pintail Road. I attended her classes as often as I was able to and painted almost daily. This was also a good opportunity to meet other people. It advanced my English at the same time. Whenever possible, I travelled with Klaus Peter. He visited hospitals in Atlanta and drove to Chattanooga, Tennessee. We flew to Miami together when he had to attend conventions there. I loved the palm trees, the pools at the motels, and the many different cuisines. We also became good friends with Nate Block who lived in Miami.

1970 Apollo 13

During the summer of 1970, Klaus Peter's parents came to visit us while we lived in Jonesboro. During their stay, Klaus Peter had to go on a brief business trip. My father-in-law said all of a sudden, "I would like to drink a beer!" Coming from Germany, he had missed a good beer. I sent him to the nearby 7-Eleven store. He arrived home happily with a case of beer. He opened a can and looked forward to have a cool beer for a change. However, when he had opened the first can and tried to drink from it, he called out, "What is that? It tastes like medicine!" To his dismay, he had purchased root beer instead of regular beer. He was so disappointed.

1971 Pentagon Papers published

After three years staying in the United States and living in Jonesboro, Georgia, on the Tara Plantation according to the novel *Gone with the Wind,* I became pregnant. Our three years had come to a close and we were supposed to leave the country and return to Germany. I got concerned when I realized this. Klaus Peter and I had a discussion what our next step should be. Christel Lawson gave me the name of her gynecologist, and Eva, another German girl from Wiesbaden, used the same doctor's office. My doctor, Dr. Glisson, was one of the first doctors who rescued Jews and other inmates from the Dachau concentration camp at the end of World War II, as I learned this from Christel Lawson.

Klaus Peter and I said to each other, "We have a house and we are expecting. Let's stay a little longer in the United States." There was now the issue with the visa, which was for three years. Klaus Peter inquired about our situation. He was able to prove that he has a trade that is needed in the United States. We were allowed to stay. So we applied for the Green Card for both of us. This process involved a complete physical, which was performed by Dr. Blumberg in Atlanta, and a background check. Upon receipt of the Green Card, this gave us the official status to remain in the United States.

One day, Jessie Carden surprised me greatly. She had invited me over to her house. I had no second thoughts because we stopped by at her house often. While I was there, friends arrived with wrapped presents. I wondered whether it was Jessie's birthday, but I have nothing to give to her. She then offered everyone some pink punch. I could have stayed on that sweet punch and being pregnant, I was craving bacon and sweets all the time. I still see myself sitting in a soft and comfy chair. Suddenly, I was instructed to open presents and all those invited guests watched me. Some of them I had met before. I wondered why me. When I carefully ripped off the paper and saw all these baby items, I was unable to say a word. For me, I thought. This was all new to me. It was not the custom in Germany. I found this awesome of Jessie and all the people who came and had bought a gift for me. I appreciated every present for my unborn child. I thanked everyone for being so kind to me.

My pregnancy was uneventful. At the Georgia Baptist Hospital in Atlanta, just before the delivery of my baby, I was asked by the doctor whether I wanted to sleep or not. I said "Yes, I like to sleep." I'm sure that it was not a deep sleep, but just sedation. When I woke up and saw Klaus Peter, I said to him in German, "We have a little boy." He said, "I know." **It was Friday, June 11, 1971.** There was another girl in the same room.

She had steady male visitors. They walked in barefoot, looked uncombed, but none was the father of the newborn child. I found this very strange and felt sorry for the mother. I was discharged the following day. I didn't nurse my little boy because of my medication, so I decided to place him on the Similac formula, the one they had started him on in the hospital.

His pediatrician in Jonesboro was Dr. Kim. My next door neighbor drove me to Dr. Kim when Klaus Peter was on the road. The time had come that I needed to get my driver's license. I enrolled in a driving school. One day, I was sitting behind the wheel and turned right at a STOP sign without coming to a full stop. There was no oncoming traffic. My instructor freaked out telling me you cannot do this. I assumed that was the way they drove in Germany, and it must be the same here. As soon as I had my license, we purchased a chocolate brown Gremlin. I liked that car. It was rather small but had a lot of power.

A brand-new life had begun. I wanted to give our little boy the same closeness and satisfaction as those who got nursed on their mother's breast. I placed him on my breast and gave him the bottle. He loved to eat and was a good infant. When he was a few months old, his body twitched occasionally. I did mention this to Dr. Kim. He informed me to watch it and let him know if it should continue or get worse. He would order an EEG to get a diagnosis. I kept a close watch on him but it disappeared.

When he was six months old we flew to Germany. He was baptized Christmas 1971 in the St. Bartholomew Church in Kirschhausen. My sister, Marianne, was his Godmother, and Pfarrer Scharf (Pastor Scharf) baptized him. I enjoyed seeing my family in Germany. My nieces and nephews had grown quite a bit since we had left. We stayed with Klaus Peter's parents who showed a lot of pride having a grandson by telling everybody that we flew home for their grandson's baptism. We stopped by at the Siemens headquarter in Erlangen, where we got our free medical and dental check-ups.

When we returned to Georgia, things started to change for me. When Klaus Peter worked locally, he was invited to Emory University in Atlanta and studied five hour long open heart surgeries. At other times, he observed similar procedures on infants and young children.

1972 Nixon visits China
          Munic Olympics massacre

I felt lonely when he traveled, especially at night. I visited Edith Patrick often. She lived on Pintail Road and was from Bavaria, Germany. Edith had two young boys. Soon after, a friend surprised and donated us an

Airedale Terrier. We named him Nosey. He dug holes in our backyard and disappeared in them. When our son was around three, he would also disappear in those close to two feet deep holes. At our next trip to Miami we took our son along. He met Nate Block. Mr. Block was so generous and purchased for our son United States Savings Bonds.

1973   Yom Kippur War
      Salvador Allende overthrown in Chile

Robby Lawson came over to our house almost every Sunday. Klaus Peter taught him things, gave him electronic items to play with, and he just seemed to enjoy being with us. He was a very pleasant teenager. The sad part about Robby was that he died of cancer at such a young age.

1974   Watergate—Nixon resigns

In 1974, when we went on a trip to Germany, we struggled what to do with Nosey. Our veterinarian had no boarding. I asked Edith Patrick whether she would be able to feed Nosey daily. During the day she could stay in the backyard and at night be kept in the garage. Nosey had other thoughts. She damaged all the doors, got out, and walked all over Bonanza, our subdivision. I don't understand why we didn't think of another solution before we left for Germany.

One afternoon, Nosey ran away and got hit on the head by a car on Tara Boulevard. From that time on, her intelligence was no longer the same.

On weekdays, I packed lunch with drinks and our son into the car. I also loaded our water raft into the car and we spent hours at the Tara Beach. It was a lot of fun to go with my son on top of the raft in the water. My skin got really brown. I never had a dark skin in Germany.

In the house behind our backyard lived the little girl, Angela. I think she was about nine. She sometimes came over to our house and stayed for a while. It bothered me that her daddy seemed to swat her, but I wasn't sure. We heard from time to time the girl's crying voice, "Daddy, no! Daddy, no!" I always wondered what she could have done that her father was so rough on her. Where was the mother? Later on, it dawned on me that I probably could have done something about it or found out more about the situation. Maybe he was an abusive father.

1975   President Ford escapes assassination attempt

We also met the von Tschirschky Family. They lived on the other side of town in North Atlanta. They used to be both German nationals. When Maria expected her second child, she asked me whether I could take care of her daughter, Elizabeth, for three days while she stayed in the hospital. We took care of their daughter and we both enjoyed the little girl. As a thank you gesture, Maria presented me a book about a little boy. The Weigl Family, Klaus Peter knew Walter from his time in Erlangen, moved to North Atlanta coming from Arizona with their two children, Harald and Claudia. We visited each other often. Soon after, Walter was transferred to the Siemens headquarter of the United States, to Iselin, New Jersey.

1976   Montreal Olympics
Jimmy Carter elected president

For a while I experienced a low point in my life and felt unhappy. Life didn't seem to offer me anything. I had enrolled our son in the United Methodist preschool for two days a week. He used to speak only German. It was not an easy start for him. He soon refused to speak German. He had friends, Travis and Andy, to play with, and a little boy from across the street. Something was missing in my life. There was a Catholic Mission Church in Jonesboro, but I had no intention to visit that church. My sister, Marianne, and brother-in-law, Fridolin, presented me with a crucifix as a gift for our wedding. This crucifix was hanging in our bedroom above the white dresser. One morning, I lay down on top of the bed in the bedroom while our son was in school. I felt sorry for myself. It seemed that I was searching for some kind of answer. All of a sudden, it felt like someone guided me to look at that crucifix hanging on the wall, and while gazing at the cross, the head of the Christ fell to the side. I heard inside me the words, "I also died for you".

This wake-up call brought me back on my feet. I made an appointment with the priest of that Mission Church, St. Philip Benizi, and asked for the Sacrament of Confession. From that time on, I knew where I belonged and that my Catholic faith was still the same as yesterday and long time ago. I ordered from Germany religion books to teach our son the faith because we spoke at home German. Later on, I went regularly to the Christ the King Cathedral in Atlanta for confession and attended Mass at St. Philip Benizi Church.

I drove with our son every morning on the days he did not attend school to the 9:00 a.m. Mass at St. Philip Benizi Church. He was the only small child and always brought the gifts to the altar. Fr. Paul Berny, the assistant priest at that time, was sometimes afraid the way he looked at my son that he would drop the glass containers but it never happened.

At one time, I met Archbishop Donnellan at a special function and I got to chat with him. He had asked me when I came to the United States. I told him in

1968. His answer was, "Oh, you are a veteran!" He was a gentle and likeable man.

In 1977, I enrolled our son in the Lillie E. Suder Elementary School on Lake Jodeco Road in Jonesboro. He was doing well. When he was in second grade, I started to prepare him for his First Holy Communion. Father John Kieran was the pastor of St. Philip Benizi Church. I was really happy to pass on my faith and seeing our son receive Holy Communion. I invited Peggy, a friend from the church community, to join us for a luncheon after the First Communion Mass. We went to the Abbey restaurant on Ponce De Leon Street in Atlanta, which is now no longer in existence.

Our son's First Holy Communion, 04/21/1979, St. Philip Benizi Church, Jonesboro, Georgia

We attended almost every year the Christmas Mass at the Monastery of the Holy Spirit in Conyers, Georgia. The monks are Cistercians monks who follow the rule of St. Benedict, ora et labora (pray and work). Once, a tornado raced with full force through Conyers, but left almost everything untouched.

1978   Pope John Paul II becomes pope

Shortly before Pentecost, Fr. Berny, assistant priest at St. Philip Benizi Church, asked me whether I would read in front of the congregation the Reading for Pentecost in German, others would read along in another language. He wanted for us to have the experience as it happened on the first Pentecost. The people understood one another even they spoke in different languages. I didn't feel comfortable at all standing in front of the congregation. I approached Fr. Berny whether my husband would be able to do it but told him that he is Lutheran. He agreed.

During the summer of 1978, while vacationing in Germany, the three of us drove to Italy and visited Rome, Assisi, Cascia, Venice, and other places of interest. In Rome, my dress had a partially open back and the guard would not let me enter St. Peter's Basilica. A stranger offered me her jacket that I could go in. I was touched by her generosity and trust. I was very much taken in by this Italian Renaissance church in Vatican City, designed principally by Donato Bramante, Michelangelo, Maderno, and Bernini. I felt the greatness of Christendom. It is the burial site of St. Peter, one of Christ's apostles, and also the first Pope. We visited the Colosseum, also known as the Flavian Amphitheater in the center of the city of Rome. It is built of concrete and sand and is the largest amphitheater ever built. The Colosseum could hold between 50.000 – 80,000 spectators. It was used for gladiatorial contests, animal hunts, executions, and more. It is partially ruined and is a popular tourist attraction. Also, each Good Friday the Pope leads a torch lit "Way of the Cross" procession that starts at the Colosseum. We visited Venice, boarded a gondola, and used those narrow street water ways, where my sun glasses were blown into the water. We greeted and fed the many doves in front of St. Mark's Basilica. The interior is graced with mosaics and icons. Italy has many outstanding basilicas.

We continued on to Assisi and Cascia, where St. Rita's, my name's sake, incorruptible body can be viewed. St. Rita is also called the Saint of the Impossible. Her life was quite heroic and I'm proud to be named after her. Assisi was the home of St. Francis. My granddaughter, Malinda, chose St. Francis as her Confirmation name.

1979 USSR invades Afghanistan
Three Mile Island nuclear incident
Iran hostage crisis begins

Klaus Peter was informed that he needs to relocate to the head quarter of Siemens in Iselin, New Jersey. This meant to sell our house we so loved and taking our son out of school. He was in third grade. The front of our house was adorned by a flame-red Pyracantha shrub, which grew into all directions. I had gotten attached to this. I was very fond of the huge back yard. I cherished everything about Georgia. The people were so easy-going and friendly. With sad feelings, we put our house on the market and sold it in no time with a big win.

1980   Moscow Olympics
       Ronald Reagan becomes U.S. President

Arriving in New Jersey, life was not as easy as in Georgia. It was much more crowded, more expensive, and the people were less friendly. Since Walter Weigl lived with his family already in Edison, New Jersey, we soon found a house that we could afford and not far from the Weigl family. It had also a big yard around the house toward Pine Street and Vineyard Road. In the front yard flowered a light pink, large magnolia shrub. Its strong, sweet scent I would have liked to have as my cologne. There was a backyard behind the two car garage with a huge oak tree right in the middle. Klaus Peter took the tree down but had to leave part of the trunk in place because the bottom part of the trunk was supported in the middle with steel. It was the size of a small coffee table. This came in handy when we had company. It looked inviting with a table cloth on it and had enough room for drinks. Later on, we added a gooseberry bush to the existing bushes in the backyard, which our German friends, Gerd and Ute Rohleder, offered us; however, before we got to enjoy the gooseberries, the birds had consumed them. The kitchen cabinets were painted in a screaming pink, and I wanted a more modern looking kitchen, so we replaced the kitchen with light oak. The tub in the bathroom was old and dirty looking. We needed to replace that, too, and the carpet throughout. Since we had sold our house in Georgia with a big win, we were able to make our new home according to our liking.

Claudia Weigl already attended the Lincoln Elementary School. We decided to enroll our son at the same school. It was also the closest. Soon we learned that New Jersey schools operated quite differently. Our son was forced to repeat the third grade because he didn't know how to write cursive. He was not taught about it in Georgia. The New Jersey school curriculum was ahead compared to Georgia. Our son stayed there for a while. We decided to take him out and register him at the St. Francis Elementary School in Metuchen, which became also our parish.

For one year I taught a religion class for the parish children who did not attend St. Francis School. I enjoyed the children especially when they asked question. These third-graders were a lot of fun. Our son prospered while attending St. Francis School. He learned to play the flute, and later on, he practiced on the pipe organ with Mr. John Novik as his instructor. Msgr. Turtora was pastor of the Cathedral Parish.

In 1980, when Liz Mahoney and I met, she immediately took me into her heart and the same happened to me. I meant a lot to her and she meant a lot to me. We were soul mates. She could have been my mother because she was much older. She loved to paint rocks with a spiritual flavor and sold them at the Charismatic prayer meeting. I still have a lot of her mail she sent to me. She passed on long ago, but we are still connected. I pray that she is at a place of rest. I had lost contact with her when she entered a nursing home. Her life was filled with sorrow. Her son-in-law committed suicide and left her daughter with four small children. Liz and John sold their house to support their daughter. They moved into an apartment and paid rent. I never realized how much I meant to her until later on in a note I treasure.

After we had settled down in New Jersey, I found an excellent neurologist in Iselin. I sat down and searched the papers for a part time job in Edison. The Montessori School in Edison was hiring. I applied and got the part-time job. This was ideal for me. I loved children, and the ride to the Montessori School was not too far. But

I realized soon that many things looked suspicious. As I found out later, the owner didn't have a license. The building needed to be cleared and we moved into a basement of a church. We didn't stay there for long because there was no fire exit. The owner of the so called Montessori School got evicted. It was disgusting. I didn't want to get involved in matters which were not my fault, so I left that place. I loved working with the little ones and felt sorry for them. It was not fair to endanger them in any way.

1981 Iran hostage crisis ends
AIDS first identified

In 1981, after I had resigned from the Montessori School, I looked into programs Middlesex County Community College in Edison offered. I enrolled in a course to become a licensed Family Day Care Provider. After completion and receiving my certification, I opened my home as a licensed Family Day Care Home. It was ideal for me because I was able to work from home, and when my son arrived after school, he didn't come to an empty house. I had a flourishing business and was well respected by my clients and in the community. I enjoyed the relationships I had with them. Because of my experience and training at the doctor's office in Germany, I felt comfortable to take in a severely handicapped little girl. Her brother was also in my care. My clients invited me to their homes for their children's birthday parties. I had various nationalities in my care. They served quite delicious, home-cooked meals.

Klaus Peter approached us with a plan to visit Holland. We liked the idea. Our first trip was to Germany. We stayed there for a few days and then continued on to Amsterdam. Amsterdam is the capital of the Netherlands. It is known for its artistic heritage, elaborate canal system and narrow houses with gabled facades, legacies of the city's 17th-century Golden Age. Its Museum District houses the Van Gogh Museum, works by Rembrandt and Vermeer at the Rijksmuseum, and modern art at the Stedelijk. Cycling is key to the city's character, and there are numerous bike paths. After spending a night in a hotel on the top floor near the canal side, we continued on to Rotterdam. Our son was taken by the many windmills in the country side. We purchased a miniature windmill to take home to the United States, including a wooden clog. Rotterdam is a major port city in the Dutch province of South Holland. The Maritime Museum's vintage ships and exhibits trace the city's seafaring history. The 17th century Delfshaven neighborhood is home to shopping at the side of the canal and Pilgrim Fathers Church, where pilgrims worshipped before sailing to America. After being almost completely reconstructed following

WWII, the city is now known for bold, modern architecture. I had a friend who was a religious Brother and lived in Steyl, Holland. Steyl is best known as a monastery village. Father Arnold Jansen founded the Divine Word Missionaries in the 1870s. The congregation is active in more than 70 countries, including the United States. We met with my friend, spent the night there, visited the main church, and learned more about their worldwide missionary activities. When I still lived at home in Germany before I got married, we used to get their monthly magazine. For many years, I continued with a subscription of *Die Stadt Gottes* (*The City of God*) coming to my home in the United States.

1982   Falkland Islands invaded by Argentina

I took a training to become a Eucharistic Minister. Deacon Bob Gellentien and I drove every other Saturday to the JFK Medical Center in Edison and brought Holy Communion to the patients. It was always a satisfying experience to be with the sick. We both belonged to the Charismatic Movement at the cathedral. Every Thursday we attended the charismatic prayer meeting, which included praying in tongues, interpretation of tongues, prophecy, laying on of hands, and prayers for healing. The songs were always so uplifting. My favorite song was *Our God reigns* - Words &

Music: Leonard E. Smith, 1974; arranged by Thomas E. Fettke & Stephen Beddia

1983   U.S. Embassy in Beirut bombed
1984   Indira Gandhi assassinated

In 1983 and 1984, I decided to take more classes to improve my English. I also enrolled in painting classes at the Metuchen High School and took instructions in flower design from a Japanese woman. The feeling and the design of the Japanese culture has always caught my attention. Soon my house was filled with flower arrangements. I donated several pieces to the John F. Kennedy Medical Center, where I had to undergo previously a few minor surgeries. My paintings were accepted by the Metuchen Fair and received ribbons. At that time, I painted only realistically or copied pieces of masters. As a child, I doodled a little on and off, but didn't see anything special in it. After painting for a while, I realized that painting will stay with me. It is relaxing and enjoyable at the same time.

Klaus Peter's colleague offered us a flight over Manhattan by night, using his own plane. I was so excited. However, I will never forget that plane ride. I'm not sure whether his colleague wanted to show off, or it was typical that with every turn he made it felt like the end is near. This was like an end of life experience, even though I don't know what that will be like. I definitely thought that my end had come and this plane will never make it down to the ground in one piece. I couldn't look out of the window any longer. In the beginning, I watched from above the millions of lights below. When he took turns or whatever he did, I got frozen up and stared at the floor in the plane. Never again will I board a small plane.

Once a month I attended a healing Mass at a missionary center in Somerset, New Jersey. I don't know whether it was a mistake or a learning experience. One of the foreign priests held seminars. They were more centered toward New Age and not Christ centered. I struggled greatly with my faith until I decided that my Catholic faith is the one I must follow. I had found my way out of something dangerous. I made mistakes in my life which I no longer regret because I learned from them.

1985 Famine in Ethiopia

During the summer of 1985 our son vacationed in Germany. Klaus Peter and I remained in the United States. We visited San Francisco, the Fisherman's Wharf, the Golden Gate Bridge, Lombard Street, Napa Valley, and Yosemite National Park. It was an enjoyable time for both of us, but most of all the San Francisco sour dough bread was so delicious that I could have lived on that.

Our son was confirmed in 1985 at the St. Francis of Assisi Cathedral in Metuchen by Bishop Theodore McCarrick, the first bishop of the Diocese of Metuchen. I had invited my friend Liz Mahoney for a little celebration at our house.

A few months later, our son developed tic like symptoms in his face. Klaus Peter and I got concerned whether he had the Gilles de la Tourette Syndrome. We drove to New York City and met with a professor who specialized in this illness. He ruled it out and we were grateful for that. However some other symptoms like forgetting the homework became an issue which pointed toward ADD. I purchased the Feingold cookbook and changed our diet around. Also, my husband and I decided that he should see a psychologist for a while to assist him with those critical teenage years. I had developed some anxiety and sought the counsel of the same doctor.

1986 Chernobyl accident
         Challenger shuttle explodes upon takeoff

I attended quite a few retreats on weekends in order to get away to refresh myself and seek spiritual renewal. One of the places was the Cenacle Retreat

House in Highland Park where I stayed from Friday to Sunday. I also went once to the Franciscan Friars of the Atonement in Graymoor, Garrison, New York. Fr. Benedict Groeschel, now deceased, attended our prayer meeting in Metuchen once. He was well known and Mother Angelica from Eternal Word Television Network and St. Teresa of Calcutta were among his close friends. I also visited often Mount Saint Mary House of Prayer in Watchung, New Jersey. I recall Sister Eileen and Sister Mary Jo to this day. At the time of writing about this, I live no longer in New Jersey for the past 25 years. The Sisters are still there. They just have aged like me. I found them on Facebook and we communicated with one another. I remember the forest which surrounded the House of Prayer. The inside decorations are still as rustic as they used to be when I was going there. I'm grateful that I had this opportunity to visit the House of Prayer for a while.

1987   DNA first used to convict criminals
Black Monday on New York Stock Exchange (NYSE)

We drove more than once to Lancaster County, Pennsylvania. Once we vacationed there. The Amish people attracted me. The history of the **Amish** church began with a schism in Switzerland within a group of Swiss and Alsatian Anabaptists in 1613 led by Jakob Ammann.

Those who followed Ammann became known as Amish. In the early 18th century, many Amish and Mennonites emigrated from Switzerland to Pennsylvania for a variety of reasons. In Pennsylvania, we watched them build their houses, and they sat in the evening in the garden. Many family members joined them while they discussed the day's happenings. They also shared their meal and conversed in the German language. We watched the children walk to school to their rather small school houses. They cultivate their farms with their own sweat. What I enjoyed the most was their buggies with the horses in front. Paradise and Intercourse are my favorite towns. Paradise has a covered bridge, an old mill, a lot of Amish farmlands, and great food. Intercourse has many unique shops and is also surrounded by farmland. The way they dress is also noteworthy. For many years I had ordered from them some of their homemade specialties. *Handkaese* (a special type of cheese) was our all time favorite. We enjoyed it while still living in Germany.

1988   Pan Am Flight 103 bombed over Lockerbie
          U.S. and Canada reach free trade agreement

In 1988, I attended a Billy Graham Crusade at Madison Square Garden. This was an awesome experience seeing thousands of people attending and being on fire for the Lord. When I learned about Fr. DiOrio, I accompanied a group of people who went on a bus tour to Connecticut to see this priest who had the gift of healing. It seemed that New Jersey was more in tune with the gifts of the Holy Spirit, but this is not the case.

The three of us travelled often to New York City to attend musicals. Peter Pan, Evita, and some others I found quite impressive. We participated in the great celebrations on July 4, 1986, with an address of President Reagan aboard the USS John F. Kennedy and a 30-minute fireworks-display and concert, scored and conducted by Joe Raposo. This was the highlight of the night. It was the largest fireworks display in American history and at the same time the largest in the world. The display included 22,000 aerial fireworks, launched from 30 barges and other vantage points, in addition to 18,000 set pieces. It was co-produced by four family-owned fireworks firms, namely the Zambelli, Grucci, Santore, and Sousa families. The trains were in operation day and night, back and forth, and all rides were free of charge. We barely got a standing spot on our return home to New Jersey.

1989 Berlin Wall falls
Tiananmen Square
Exxon Valdez spills millions of gallons of oil

We usually spent New Year's Eve with the Weigl Family at their house and enjoyed a good dinner with champagne at midnight. In the meantime, Walter has died of lung cancer, and Margit lives in a home for assisted living. We were very surprised to receive a Christmas card from her. Claudia, her daughter, informed me some time ago that her mother started having the Alzheimer disease when she was 70 years old.

Our three nieces, Gabi Maria, Evi, and Barbara from Germany spent three weeks with us in Edison, New Jersey. They enjoyed every minute staying with us. We visited New York City, Lady Liberty, and enjoyed a Manhattan Island Cruise. This was their highlight. The girls carried little bottles of cologne around. Our son, not used to girls or he was jealous, wasted their cologne. The bathroom had the loudest smell. Its fragrance was overwhelming. When they had returned to Germany, all three girls would constantly write to us. I treasure their letters, which I still carry in a special folder. Each one shared their own pain being back in Germany. According to their letters, they must have cried a lot. When our son graduated from High School, my sister Marianne, our son's Godmother, arrived with her son, Andreas. It was a wonderful experience for them to see each student with his cap, gown, and tassel walking up the isle receiving his diploma.

During their stay in New Jersey, Harald Weigl got married to Shirley. We all were invited, including my sister and Andreas. They had their wedding at a building which looked like a castle. Andreas had asked me, "Are these royals?" I denied it.

After we had put Nosey asleep because of constant bladder infections and as a result wetted all over the place, we decided to get another small dog. There was a breeder in Scotch Plains who bred Yorkshire Terriers. We took a trip up there, and I immediately fell in love with a Yorkie puppy. We purchased one and named him Maxie. I trained him that he would make his duty outdoors. Looking back at the type of training I was instructed to do by the seller was in my eyes ridiculous. I was supposed to give him a suppository that he would do his duties outdoors. I followed the instructions, but I wouldn't do this again. Maxie had quite a character and was not afraid of big dogs. One of our neighbors had a dog that ran back and forth in their backyard. When he saw Maxie, he got very frenzy and barked non-stop. Maxie walked peacefully over, lifted his leg on the other dog's nose, then would walk on. Maxie loved to steal the pacifiers of my Day Care children and would use them for himself. Maybe he was jealous of my Day Care kids. He lived up to 19 years and died later on in Colorado in the middle of the roses in our backyard. This was always his favorite place.

Our Yorkshire Terrier, Maxie, with a stolen pacifier

Before we got Maxie, we had adopted another dog, but only for a brief time. He was a mixed breed and looked like a little pig. His fur felt like straw. I probably thought that I would get a little pig. I remember our ride when we brought him home. I held him in my lap and after a while, he threw up all over my pants. We had a sunroom attached to our house. It had carpet as a floor covering. In no time he had ripped out the carpet in the sunroom. He was constantly up to something. I was busy with the children in my care and couldn't give him my full attention. Unfortunately, we couldn't keep him.

Our son owned a parakeet. He always vocalized "Polly good bird!" When he died, we purchased another one. To our delight, he started saying the same words.

1990   Lech Walesa becomes first president of Poland
      Nelson Mandela freed

While we lived in New Jersey, there were many young Vietnamese refugees arriving in New Jersey. I questioned myself whether this would be something for us to consider, to adopt one of these youngsters. I discussed this with my husband. He did not share my idea. I attended a retreat on discernment, and I wrote a letter to Mother Teresa of Calcutta. In 1990, to my surprise, I received a letter back from Mother Teresa with her own signature on it. While writing this, Mother Teresa is now Saint Teresa of Calcutta. She died in 1997 and was canonized in 2016 by Pope Frances. Her letter to me is not a first class relic, alone her thoughts and experiences in this letter, her handwriting, and her prayers for me are very special to me.

We travelled back to Germany every two to three years. A trip to the Austrian state of Salzburg and Kaprun is quite an adventure. The presence of the Kitzsteinhorn Glacier dominates Kaprun. This gigantic mountain with its perpetual ice is worth a trip. We drove through Zell am See just before dusk when suddenly through one of the villages trotted a herd of cows on their way home. Around their neck, they wore the most colorful neck bands. Large bells were attached to them and their clang stopped all onlookers. The cars turned to the side until all the cows had passed by.

While we lived in Edison, New Jersey, every Tuesday evening I had a group of friends gather at my house. We listened to spiritual tapes and music, enjoyed our friendship, and prayed for the needs of others. These evenings were filled with much peace. We all looked forward to Tuesday. I continued these gatherings in Highlands Ranch, Colorado, while Klaus Peter lived in North Carolina.

In the summer of 1990, my husband's parents visited us in New Jersey. Klaus Peter came up with the plan to visit Canada and the Niagara Falls. With great excitement we all agreed. We packed our suit cases and drove up to the Finger Lakes. It is a group of eleven long, narrow, roughly north-south lakes in a region called the Finger Lake region in Central New York in the United States. It is defined as a bioregion and is a popular tourist destination. Our next step was the Niagara Falls. Niagara Falls is the collective name for three waterfalls, the *Horseshoe Falls,* the *American Falls,* and *the Bridal Veil Falls.* We took a tour in the boat below the falls and had to wear a black rain coat, but we still got wet. It was an awesome experience to see these wide masses of water flowing down. The falls are not extremely high but wide. The following day we continued on to Corning in New York and visited the *Corning Museum of Glass.* It is dedicated to the art, history, and science of glass. This was quite impressive, too.

When we returned home from the trip, my mother-in-law asked immediately, "Let's play Monopoly!" She had fallen in love with this board game.

1991   Collapse of USSR
        Operation Desert Storm in Persian Gulf

At the end of 1991, Klaus Peter was informed by his boss that he would be transferred to Siemens Medical in Colorado. This meant that we must place our house on the market again, close my Day Care business, break up friendships, and much more. I realized that we lived twelve years in Georgia, and it had been twelve years in New Jersey. Is twelve a magic number for us? I had a final get together with my friends who attended the weekly gatherings at my house. It was difficult for me to part from them. Some of them are no longer among the living. We then decided at the beginning of 1992 to vacation in Colorado and investigate our future home to be. We took a flight to Denver, got a glimpse of the Rocky Mountains, and visited Siemens. Klaus Peter's colleagues invited us to the Trail Dust, a fun and tasty experience in dining. The following day, the three of us drove to Mesa Verde National Park. The park with its cliff dwellings offered us a spectacular look into the lives of the Pueblo Indians who lived there for over 700 years, from AD 600 to AD 1300. Today, the park protects close to 5,000 known archeological sites, including 600 cliff dwellings. These sites are some of the most notable and best preserved in the United States. Driving out there left us a good impression of Colorado. We experienced sunshine every day, friendly people, and more space all over than in New Jersey. We discovered some new and interesting food and great varieties. I really enjoyed the Trail Dust with its Western band, a long slide, cutting off the tie when it was your birthday, and the steaks were excellent. Unfortunately, Trail Dust is no longer around in our area.

Whenever we travelled to Germany, we always took trips with my sisters, Irene and Agnes, and their spouses. At one time, the six of us walked all the way up to the Breitfussalm while vacationing in Hinterglemm, Austria. After eating a hearty luncheon, it was time to return to Hinterglemm. We were too tired to walk back. However, Agnes was always so afraid to enter a cable car. She rather walked, but nobody wanted to walk back, so she was forced to face her anxiety and step into the cable car. She survived the ride down.

At the Breitfussalm with my sisters, Agnes and Irene

Once a week I attended Bible study in Edison at Ruth Inglis' house with the assistance of Father Bill Halbing. He always tried to speak the little German he knew and said to me, "Wie gehts!" (How are you doing?) Some other friends, including Liz Mahoney, always joined this group. Later on, when Ruth had passed on, we attended Father Bill Halbing's Bible study on Sundays at St. Francis of Assisi Cathedral. Father Bill is still very active to this day and well known all over. He is a lively speaker and knows the Word of God, the Bible, inside out. He is also fluent in Spanish and is stationed in the Diocese of Newark, New Jersey. After our move to Colorado, I met him several times in Colorado Springs, where I attended conferences and he was a guest speaker.

1992   Official end of the Cold War

The year 1992 had arrived. It was also the year for our transfer to Colorado. I remember when the moving van arrived. Our son's car was loaded into the van and then mine while my friend, Margit Weigl, watched and cried. It was difficult for her to see us leave. We spent twelve years together in New Jersey and before some time in Georgia. In Edison, they lived basically just around the corner from us on Dundar Road, while we lived on Pine Street. As soon as the movers left, our next trip was to the attorneys to finalize the sale of the house. They used a ton of paper for this transaction. When they had finished typing out everything, they had made a mistake and placed our name as the buyer and the other party as the seller. We had already planned to be on the road, but it took them forever to correct their mistake. It was difficult to leave New Jersey where I had so many friends, but it was good that we took our vacation in Colorado, so we knew what to expect. We had purchased a house that was beyond our dreams. It received last minute touch ups so we could move in at our arrival in Colorado. Maxie was riding with us in the car and when we arrived in Colorado, we stayed for a few days in a hotel until the house was ready and we received our papers to be the homeowner of our dream house. As soon as the furniture arrived, we were ready to move in. Our brand new house was in Highlands Ranch on 9979 South Cottoncreek Drive. The basement was one large dance floor. The first floor had a large kitchen, breakfast nook, family room, dining-room, study, and formal living room, and bathroom. The upstairs had three guest bedrooms, full guest bath, master bedroom, master bathroom, and a large walk-in closet. I immediately started planning what kind of flowers I wanted to see in our front yard and what trees, if any, should be planted in the huge backyard. The kitchen nook had a wide glass door from where you walked out on the deck and down the stairs to the backyard.

During the war in Bosnia-Herzegovina in 1992-1995, I wrote a novel about four Muslim children who had lost all family members. They had to endure many hardships and escaped the war. They found their way to Heidelberg, Germany, where a childless couple adopted them. I didn't pursue to get this novel published.

A few days prior to our first Christmas in Colorado in 1992, I received mail from my friend Liz Mahoney in New Jersey. I opened it, but since there was no letter included except a brochure, I didn't read it. Also, St. Thomas More, my new parish, had offered four days prior to Christmas the one man play *"St. John of the Cross, the Living Flame of Love"*, played by Leonardo de Fillipe. I didn't want to miss this and attended the play. I cannot describe how deeply touched I was watching how incredibly spiritual Leonardo de Fillipe personified St. John of the Cross. It was so authentic that it touched the core of my being. On Christmas Day we attended the 10:30 a.m. Mass at St. Thomas More Church. After the Offertory, I was carried away for a second or two while I seemed to dream or heard the message, "I want for you to be a Carmelite." I still didn't think much about it, but didn't forget or put it aside either.

After Christmas I opened the envelope from Liz Mahoney again and looked at the brochure. This is not like Liz that she doesn't put a note to it, I thought. I browsed through the brochure and found three addresses in there where I could inquire about Secular Carmelites. I chose the address in Connecticut and requested more information. I was referred to Seattle, Washington. That was the beginning of my Carmelite journey. I started out as an Isolate and received monthly lessons by mail and sent a written response back. After six months, a few professed members from the Denver and Colorado Springs area got together, and this became the genesis of the Secular Carmelite Community in Denver. After a few years, I made the temporary Promise before Father Walsh at the Jesuit Retreat House in Sedalia, Colorado. Two years later I made my Definitive Promise in the presence of Father Bill Brock at St. Dominic Catholic Church in Denver. There was a voluntary vow after one year, which I made as well. After close to ten years, the Carmelite Community of the Holy Spirit was canonically established by Rome. New members are being added all the time. At the time of my writing this, we are about ninety members. Some are still in Formation. Extended members are those who out of health reasons can no longer attend the monthly meetings. We have annual retreats at the St. Francis Retreat Center in Colorado Springs and meet monthly at St. Thomas More Catholic Church.

As soon as I was somewhat established in Colorado, I applied for my license again to operate a Family Day Care home, but this time for infants and toddlers, which meant that I could have only four children at any time. It was granted to me after six weeks. Through my Carmelite vocation, I tried harder to be more sensitive to the needs of others. After working for several months in Colorado, a 10-months old little boy got critically ill while in my care. I noticed that this infant was very different on any given day and this time was motionless lying in the crib. I called the parents. They took him to the hospital and he was diagnosed with Type I diabetes. The parents begged me to keep him. They would have trained me to give him injections, but I had a responsibility toward the other children in my care and declined.

I joined the Day Care Association, and soon afterwards, I accepted the responsibilities of the secretary and the referral. I met quite a few other Day Care providers and felt soon at home in Colorado. Also, I had met the spouses of other Siemens employees. We were invited and attended many outdoor parties. I quickly adjusted to my new home and life, and I got acquainted with Janet from down the street.

In the meantime, the few professed Secular Carmelites and myself had found a meeting place which was the Risen Christ Church in Denver. The professed members appointed me secretary and treasurer, while they instructed new members. I was no longer considered an Isolate and received my instructions from our professed members under the guidance of the provincial superior for our jurisdiction. What is the Secular Carmelite Order or what is required of its members?

The Seculars' vocation is to live the Carmelite spirituality as Seculars and not as mere imitators

of Carmelite monastic life. They practice contemplative prayer while living lives of charity in their common occupations. They profess a promise to the Order patterned on the monastic vows which guides their life. The Promise is to live according to the Rule of St. Albert and the OCDS Constitutions and to live the evangelical counsels of chastity, poverty, and obedience and the beatitudes according to their lay state of life.

Spiritually mature members receiving the recommendation of the local council of their OCDS community and the approval of their provincial superior are permitted to profess vows of chastity and obedience to their community, which are strictly personal and do not translate into a separate class of membership.

Prayer to Our Lady of Mount Carmel
Mary, my Mother, Queen Beauty of Carmel
My teacher, my model of excellence
You instruct me to suffer quietly and lovingly
To keep inner silence amidst noisy gongs
To listen to my heart's whisper
To die to my false self

How can I thank you?
How can I love you more?

You wish to remain just a mother
Pointing toward your precious Son
My Brother, my Lord and Savior

Lady of Mount Carmel
Stay with me always and everywhere
Paralyze the evil one at the hour
Of my last breath
That no injury befalls my eternal soul
Lead me safely into the heavenly Jerusalem—
The home of the Holy Trinity
And my home
Mother, for these I thank you
From the bottom of my heart. Amen

        --Rita Lulay Malsch, OCDS

But before long, bad news caused us sleepless nights. One day, when Klaus Peter arrived home from work, he announced the news I didn't want to hear. Siemens in Colorado will be closed down and we have to move to North Carolina. I just couldn't believe what I just had heard. Soon after, we also learned that our house had major problems with the foundation, which included the properties of two neighbors. We had no other choice than to file a law suit. I told Klaus Peter that I will stay in Colorado. We also were unable to sell the house under these conditions. This was not easy for both of us to undertake another move and this time to North-Carolina and in such a short time. I almost felt like a gypsy. We had to find the best solution and decide upon it. I said I remain in Colorado. He soon had to leave and looked for a house in Fuquay Farina, North Carolina. He purchased a cute little Ranch Style house with living-room, two bedrooms, kitchen and dining-room, two-car garage, and a large back- and front yard with a long driveway. It was located in a nice area. During the day, I was busy with my Day Care children. I loved my job working with infants and toddlers. The class action suit for our house was in progress. Soon we learned that the house is going to be repaired. This meant that the entire house needed to be lifted while they place piers into the ground. This was a major undertaking and I asked whether I could continue with my work and have children in the house. I never knew that a house with the size of ours could be lifted. It sure was quite an undertaking. We didn't notice any lifting when they set the house on piers. The funny part was the workers used to bring their lunches and left them outside of the house. However, a yellow Lab who lived down the street passed by daily. He must have thought that other people's lunches taste much better than what they offer me at home. Until the workers discovered who was munching their lunches, the hungry Lab had clearly no guilt feelings to feed on those delicious sandwiches.

1993   World Trade Center bombed

We again travelled to Germany for a two week vacation. We spent a day with my husband's parents in Strasbourg, France. It is the capital and largest city of the Grand Est region of France. It is located close to the German border in the historic region of Elsace. It is also the official seat of the European Parliament. We visited the Strasbourg Cathedral and the Old Town, had a French luncheon, and took a boat ride on one of the artificial waterways. Afterwards we got called by our bus driver to fill the bus again for our return home. It was an enjoyable day with great weather, fun, and good food.

When our vacation came to a close, it always happened too quickly, and as always, we had to say Hello and Good Bye to other family members like aunts and uncles, at least to those who lived close by. We were already looking forward to our next trip to Germany.

In 1993, we celebrated our 25th Wedding Anniversary. Many other couples observed their 25th and 50th Wedding Anniversary at the Immaculate Heart of Mary Church in Northglenn, Colorado. We all received a

certificate from Archbishop James Francis Stafford of
Denver. Archbishop Stafford is now Cardinal Stafford.

Our 25. Wedding Anniversary with Archbishop Stafford

August 10 – 15, 1993, was designated for World Youth Day in Denver, Colorado. The theme was *I came that they may have life, and have it to the full* (John 10:10). It was a big event for Catholic youth and 500,000+ youth participated at the closing at the Cherry Creek State Park. Pope John Paul II presided at that Mass. My parish, St. Thomas More in Centennial, was responsible for 3,000 youth from France. We housed a French priest and two French youths. Upon leaving, the priest left me his own cross he wore around his neck. He spoke briefly about the Catholic Church in France. Priests don't have an easy life or much to say. One of the youth who stayed at my house did go to the Mile High Flea Market instead of going to the programs the church offered. This was disappointing to me. I made daily food packages for them. It seemed to me that it was more important to him to get to the United States than attending religious programs. However it was all over a good experience to have three foreign nationals at my house for a few days. Our son was in charge of the sound at St. Thomas More Church. August 14, 1993, Aaron Jean-Marie Lustiger, who accompanied the French delegation, blessed our new adoration chapel at St. Thomas More Church. He was a French Cardinal of the Roman Catholic Church, adviser to Pope John Paul II, and Archbishop of Paris from 1981 until his retirement in 2005. He was born to Jewish parents in Paris, France. His parents were Ashkenazi Jews from

Bedzin, Poland. While his mother ran a business in Paris, she was deported and murdered in September 1942 in Auschwitz-Birkenau. Cardinal Lustiger's life always touched me deeply.

I opened my Day Care at 7:10 a.m. instead of 7:00 a.m. so that I could attend the early morning Mass. I signed up for the training to become a Eucharistic Minister again. Since we had a Perpetual Adoration chapel, I also signed up for an hour to spend with the Eucharistic Lord. I received strength for being alone with my son, my work, and the daily challenges.

Since Klaus Peter lived alone in North Carolina and flew home only once a month, this situation was difficult for him. I talked to my friend, Louise Brodie, who bred and raised Yorkshire Terriers and presented her dogs in shows, whether she has a puppy available for purchase. She told me that she has three newborns. I said to her I will come by and select one. At our next phone conversation the following day, I asked Klaus Peter whether he can handle a little Yorkshire Terrier. I just wanted for him not to be so alone. He agreed with my offer. Next, I drove to Denver to meet with Louise at her place. She showed me the three little puppies whose eyes were still closed. One was making noises, almost like a bark. I picked this one and we named him Moritz. I kept Moritz for a while because he was so little and placed him in a play pen in the kitchen while I was working. He was such a cute puppy.

A flight attendant was looking for a room. While Klaus Peter was living in North Carolina, I accepted that lady into my home. I rented out our guest room and collected some income at the same time. Blanca is a nice woman and later on moved to Zephyrhills, Florida. We still have contact with one another.

Once in a while, I flew with Maxie to North Carolina. I had a travel bag for him which had flowers on the outside and looked like a regular purse. Part of the purse was a net to let the air through. Nobody realized that there was a pet inside. I administered Maxie a little Valium that he would not bark. The veterinarian prescribed it for him. It worked out perfectly. Once I spent Thanksgiving with Klaus Peter in North Carolina. The Schroeder family invited us for dinner. Klaus Peter and I had a grant time being together for a few days. On Sunday I attended Mass in St. Bernadette's Catholic Church in Fuquay Farina. The flight from Denver to Chicago and back was always fine. However, I dialed Klaus Peter from Chicago once. I used my Visa number and immediately had it stolen. I didn't know that somebody stood probably behind me or what kind of trick that person played to get my VISA number. When I had returned home, I learned what had happened and how much money he or she had stolen from my account. VISA took care of it. I received a different card with a new number. I dreaded that little plane from Chicago to Raleigh and back. Looking through the window, I saw trees and lakes. Everything was so close to the ground. They served only a bag with peanuts. This tiny plane was not my way of flying, but there was no other choice. While still living in North Carolina, and he had three more months to go before his 65th birthday and retirement, Klaus Peter was told that he can retire now. This was a German guy who probably didn't like my husband. He wanted to give him a blow in the face. An American in Iselin got involved and made sure that he receives his full retirement. Klaus Peter was then able to return to Colorado. After two long years, the ordeal of living away from home was finally over.

He had no problem selling the house in North Carolina and again with profit.

1994   Rwandan genocide
        Channel Tunnel opens

Down the street lived my good friend Janet. Janet and Franklin always invited us on Christmas Day for dinner. Their children and grandchildren were present and two other friends were invited as well.

On Christmas Day 1994, Janet handed to me a beautifully wrapped box. I removed the Christmas paper, opened the box, and then gazed at the *Christmas in Colorado Cook Book* with Recipes, Traditions and Folklore for the Holiday Season. I cherish this very much. She deserves a special place in my heart. She passed away on February 4th, 2011. My husband and I attended her funeral. Her daughter Anjanet was brave enough and delivered the eulogy about her mother. Anjanet used to have asthma and her brother had heart surgery when he was an infant. Janet always shared with me her continued concerns about her children, especially about her son Skipper, even though he no longer had any heart issues. Janet also invited me to Sorority meetings at her home, other people's homes, or restaurants, which included luncheons. The meaning of these gatherings was new to me, and Janet explained to me the purpose behind them. If family members couldn't go to college for various reasons, especially women, they increased their education through gatherings like these. The discussions included various topics. I enjoyed these meetings. I also made many new friends.

1995   Oklahoma City bombing
        Yitzhak Rabin assassinated

In 1995, Sharon Young, a fellow Secular Carmelite, and I drove to Albuquerque, New Mexico, to attend a Carmelite retreat. Father Michael Buckley, OCD, was the retreat master. On our way we made a quick stop in Santa Fe to see the Miraculous Staircase, but the chapel door was locked. It was after 5:00 p.m. We continued on to Albuquerque to arrive in time for the beginning of the retreat. I never was in close touch with Southwestern Flair. I fell in love with it and purchased at the end of the retreat a large picture. It started snowing on our way home. Sharon and I got concerned that we would not make it over the Raton Pass. We drove slowly and took turns every 45 minutes. After a while, Sharon said, "I can no longer drive, I have become snow blind." I had to take over and kept on driving. I was from that moment on responsible for the rest of the trip. It was already pitch-dark and it continued to snow. After hours of driving, we finally arrived in Colorado Springs, Colorado. However with these snowy conditions, we needed at least another hour to my house in Highlands Ranch. I had no time to worry, I needed trust, and the retreat left me with much peace. When we arrived at my place, Jim, Sharon's husband, waited already in his car. It was cold and he couldn't enter my house because my son was not home. I was grateful that we returned home safely, especially under these snowy conditions. Also, I had never driven long distances before, but there is always a first time.

Through a phone conversation with my cousin, Gerda, in Austin, Texas, I learned that Frau Dr. Berg is currently in Texas visiting a friend. I then asked Gerda for the phone number and contacted Frau Dr. Berg directly. I asked her whether she would like to spend some time with me. She agreed. On the weekend, when Klaus Peter was at home in Colorado, we picked up Frau Dr. Berg at the airport. She stayed with me for an entire week. We had a wonderful time together and shared many different things. Our family room in Highlands Ranch had huge windows. When you entered the house, your eyes walked straight to the windows. The first thing Frau Dr. Berg said when she stepped into our house, "Who is washing these windows?" When she drove with me to a drive-through bank, she said we don't have those in Germany, which I doubted. I needed a root canal treatment while she was here. She stayed with the children during my dental appointment. The dentist called me later in the day and inquired about my condition. She was so surprised and said to me, "They don't call you in Germany!" I invited her out for dinner at the Trail Dust. Our son and his girlfriend at that time, Antonella Cammarotta, joined us, too. Frau Dr. Berg enjoyed the steak and found it quite tasty. She also liked the Western flavor at this restaurant. She probably didn't remember that she had hurt me long time ago. I tried hard to forget and forgive her. We are all human beings and, at times, hurt others, myself included. Forgiving others is the hardest thing to do. I was hurt many times in my life. I think I have learned quite a bit from it. If you can rise above the hurt you must accept yourself as you are. The hurt becomes little, almost non-existent, because the person didn't know what he was doing or saying. Frau Dr. Berg died six months later while vacationing at her daughter, Karin, in Holland. I was happy that we were able to spend this week together before she passed away.

In 1995, the three of us vacationed in Germany. Our son remained in Germany with his grandparents and other family members for the rest of the summer. Klaus Peter and I tried to return back home to the States when I realized in Frankfurt at the airport that I had left my Green Card back home in the States. Without the Green Card, I was not able to enter the country. Klaus Peter flew back to the States and I stayed in Germany. Mr. Lissina, Klaus Peter's boss, was scheduled to fly to Germany a few days after Klaus Peter's arrival in the States. This came quite handy to me. Mr. Lissina took my Green Card to Germany. We met him at the Frankfurt International Airport and he handed the Green Card to me. I booked a new flight and then returned back home. It was difficult for me to stay alone in Germany. It was no longer home to me even though I was not yet an American citizen.

1996   Mad cow disease hits Britain
         Unabomber arrested

We took another trip to Germany and drove on a day trip to Colmar, France, with Irene and Agnes and their husbands. Colmar is also a town in the Alsace region of northeastern France, near the border with Germany. Its old town has cobblestone streets lined with half-timbered medieval and early Renaissance buildings. It is a city you want to visit more than once. There is so much to see and it is quite colorful. The food is typically French, and wine lovers come to the right place.

On our flight back home, the agent cut our Green Cards in Chicago and told us, if you want to become a citizen, it takes only six months. If you apply for another Green Card, it will take a year. Back home in Colorado, we decided to become citizens of the United States. We had no desire to return to Germany and live there permanently. Littleton High School offered citizenship classes. I signed up and attended those classes. I got acquainted with many foreign nationals, some spoke barely any English, but all looked forward to become citizens of this great country. Our teacher was an elderly gentleman who taught with great enthusiasm American history. His pride being an American was contagious. When I was ready, my friend Edith, she is from Lima, Peru, and made her citizenship years before me, drove me to the Immigration and

Naturalization office in Denver, Colorado, where I was tested and sworn in. I was nervous but the questions were not difficult. I answered them all correctly. I studied and prepared for that. It all happened on **January 13, 1997**. At that moment, I lost my German citizenship. It was a strange feeling, but the United States had become my home. I still love my birth country and always will, but it has changed tremendously and gone into a direction I don't appreciate. Well, the entire world is at a turning point. I probably would not feel at home in Germany anymore. Edith was so gracious and stayed with me through the entire time and drove me home as well. When I arrived back at the house in Highlands Ranch, I called and informed my three sisters in Germany.

1997   *Princess Diana dies in car crash*
       Hong Kong returned to China

When Klaus Peter lived in Colorado again, one evening we dressed up, took the light rail to Denver, and enjoyed the musical *Cats*.

At another time, we went with our friends, Edith and Anthony, and attended the musical *The Trapp Family*.

1998   India and Pakistan both test nuclear weapons

It was May 2nd, 1998, and the day had arrived when Mary, Madelaine, and I made the Definitive Promise in the Secular Order of Carmel. Father Bill Brock was the Presider.

My Definitive Promise in Carmel with Fr. Bill Brock, Mary, and Madelaine

1999 Euro becomes new European currency
JFK Jr. dies in plane accident
NATO attacks Serbia

2000 USS Cole bombed
Unclear winner in U.S. presidential election
Concorde crashes near Paris

On a hot summer day in 2000, Klaus Peter and I encountered a difficult situation. A ham operator friend said to us, "I heard that you are going to be grandparents!"

We kind of ignored it because our son lived at home and he was not going steady with someone.

November 11 came around when the door bell rang. We opened the door. In front of the door stood Jamie, a girl we had barely met, and her mother. We kind of knew how she looked like and I had warned him quite a few times. Jamie's mom started talking and said, "I want to talk to you about the kids." We still had no idea what we would soon learn. She then said, "They got a little girl two days ago." We found no words. It was a shock and not a small one. However, this child needed to be loved and cared for. As soon as they were gone, we looked at each other and didn't know exactly what to do next. Klaus Peter said to me, "Let's purchase a balloon and flowers. We will go straight over to Jamie's grandmother!" Jamie stayed with the baby at her grandmother's house. When we arrived, our son was in the garage and didn't see us coming. We went into the house and saw Jamie and the baby. There was a beautiful little girl with black hair. We handed Jamie the flowers and the balloons. Klaus Peter asked to hold the child. I was still in a state of shock, except I couldn't show it. After a few minutes our son came in. I had the feeling that he had suffered greatly. When he saw us he had tears in his eyes. He was always a somewhat sensitive child, had ADD, but he was afraid to tell us that he was a father now. He assumed that we would throw him out of the house. They got married by the Justice of the Peace. We purchased for them a condominium. Whether this was the right thing to do, I'm not sure anymore. As soon as the little girl was old enough to come to my Day Care, I was at peace that she received what she needed. Soon afterwards we filed for custody for the girl, which was quite difficult and costly. After a thorough investigation, it was granted to us. However, the situation did not end there. Soon, the girl's mother was pregnant again. A little boy, born March 18, 2004, arrived. He was born with a club foot. He needed surgeries in order to get the leg back to normal again. He had excellent doctors, and they did an awesome job with his leg. This leg is like his other one. He was a handsome, young, and lovable little boy and coped well with his condition. I sensed strange feelings inside me that the mother got bored and wanted to be free again. Whenever she decided to pick up the girl from my Day Care setting, and this was only once in a while, the child refused to go to her mother. I soon noticed that something was going seriously wrong.

2001   9/11 terrorist attacks in U.S.

Anthrax scare

Taliban regime in Afghanistan collapses

My sister, Irene with husband and their son Alexander, visited us in Highlands Ranch. We decided to drive up to the highest mountain in the Rocky Mountains in

North America, Mount Evans. I see the mountain on a daily basis, but driving up is quite another experience. We drove to Idaho Springs at 8,700 feet, turned off on Interstate 70 to 14,240 feet to the summit. We passed three life zones, ancient trees, lakes, and forest to the land above timberline. It can be 90 degrees in Denver and 40 degrees at the top of Mount Evans. Mountain goats and Bighorn Sheep greeted us on both sides of the car as we climbed to the top. It was a thrilling experience. When we reached the summit and got out of the car, we needed our sweaters. There was a small lake. At that lake grew a single marsh marigold or buttercup. Everything is under natural reserve.

The following day we packed our bags again and drove to the Yellowstone National Park. The ride alone was an adventure because for miles we didn't pass any car. We drove through Grand Teton National Park which is in the northeast of the U.S. state of Wyoming. It encompasses the Teton mountain range, the 4,000 m Grand Teton peak, and the valley called Jackson Hole. It is well visited in the summer for hiking, backcountry camping, fishing, and mountaineering. Yellowstone National Park is a nearly 3,500-square-mile wilderness recreation area atop a volcanic hot spot. Mostly in Wyoming, the park spreads into parts of Montana and Idaho, too. Yellowstone National Park features dramatic canyons, alpine rivers, lush forests, hot springs, and gushing geysers, including its most famous *Old Faithful.* It's also home to hundreds of animal species, including bears, bison, elk and antelope. My German relatives were quite impressed with the park. We also visited the U. S. State of Utah. It is a western state defined by its vast expanses of desert and the Wasatch Range Mountains. Salt Lake City is the capital. We visited the Mormon Church with its majestic temple and tabernacle, the massive dome, and the renowned choir. We continued on to the Arches National Park, which lies north of Moab, Utah. It is bordered by the Colorado River in the southeast. It is known as the site of more than 2,000 natural sandstone arches, such as the massive, red-hued Delicate Arch in the east. Long, thin Landscape Arch stands in Devil's Garden to the north. Other geological formations include Balanced Rock, towering over the desert landscape in the middle of the park. This was quite an experience for all of us. Afterwards, in one of the local restaurants nearby, I ate a grilled and well seasoned rainbow trout from the Colorado River.

2002   Bali bombings
     Moscow theatre hostage crisis

It was a sunny and promising Mother's Day. I drove home from the 10:30 a.m. Mass when suddenly on South Quebec Street a car emerged from the right.

This woman behind the wheel ran a STOP sign on her side street where she was supposed to stop and look for traffic in the street she was about to enter. She hit me on the left side of the car that I couldn't open the door. Someone who observed the accident must have called the police. I don't remember whether I called my husband or the police called him. The police officer encouraged me to go to the Emergency Room. I told the police that I'm fine, but they still urged me to do so. We also learned that this woman had too much alcohol so early in the day. We went for a Mother's Day brunch, but I said to my husband, "Let's go to the ER. I want to be told that nothing serious happened to me!" We drove to the Littleton Hospital to get checked out. I was told to take it easy the next few days. If something should come up, to return to the hospital immediately. The following day I experienced ringing in the ears and some dizziness. That was not all. New symptoms like pain in my left hip emerged, continued dizziness, ringing in the ears, and I didn't feel well at all. Soon I needed to see an orthopedic doctor. He treated me for a while until he informed me that the left hip needed to be replaced. I was struggling to keep my Day Care open. With all the doctor appointments, and it seemed that new symptoms surfaced on a daily basis, I realized that the end of running my business was fast approaching. In addition, the ringing in my ears increased, and I had to drive constantly to the ENT (ear, nose, throat) specialist at the Swedish Medical Center in Englewood. I had several treatments for my ears and the hip replacement surgery was also scheduled. My condition didn't improve, and I had to make the difficult decision to close my Family Day Care business, which I had enjoyed for 20 years. I was angry. I had so many wonderful clients over the years who really appreciated my work with their precious little ones. I searched for an attorney who offered a free half-an-hour consultation because I needed to know whether I have any chance to sue this drunk driver. I felt lost and got somewhat depressed. In the meantime, I was scheduled for the hip replacement surgery at Littleton Hospital. I lost a lot of blood during the surgery and was then transferred a day after the surgery to the Porter Hospital in Englewood where I received a blood transfusion.

2003 Columbia shuttle explosion
Iraq War begins

I enjoyed living in the house in Highlands Ranch. It was spacey. We had installed two large flower boxes on the front two window sills. Every spring we planted different flowers with varied colors in those boxes. One spring morning, there was a baby robin sitting in the box amidst the flowers. It couldn't fly yet. I got the impression that it was comfortable staying there until it was ready to be on its own. I always had a big heart for birds. One late fall day, I was outdoors and it had started getting dark when I saw two great horned owls sitting on top of the roof of our house. I wouldn't want to miss this moment and didn't run into the house to get my husband. When the two owls decided to move on, it felt like two planes flying right above me. These birds are amazing creatures.

The front of our house in Highlands Ranch

Once I was driving north on Quebec Street in Highlands Ranch when to my immense surprise I witnessed a shooting star. It had a tail and a big ball in the front. I was quite taken by this experience because it appeared that it would shoot upwards and then dive to earth with high speed. It was really bright and could not be missed. Then it shattered violently. There was not much traffic and being distracted by this could have caused an accident.

On March 18, 2003, my right hip was replaced. After this ordeal, we decided to downsize and purchase a new house with the master bedroom on the first floor. In our Highlands Ranch house, I needed to sleep in the study on the first floor because walking stairs after the left hip surgery was impossible.

After my discharge and recuperation, I decided seriously to file a lawsuit against this woman in relation to my left hip replacement. The Bell & Pollock Law Firm advertised daily on radio and in the Yellow Pages. I scheduled an appointment with Mr. Pollock. He listened to my experiences with this intoxicated lady driver on Mother's Day, my ongoing health issues, and he accepted my case. He also informed me that I had to go for a day long deposition. I let him know that I cannot sit for an entire day. He got the case rolling. I was scheduled for September 16, 2005, for spine surgery, which was covered by that lady's insurance through the law suit. I went to the hospital with a fairly good spirit, also trusted my surgeon. He spoke fluently German, had studied for a while at a German university, and his mother was from Germany. However, the pain after the surgery with spinal fusion and the following rehabilitation was so excruciating that I kept crying in bed for Mama and Papa. I had the feeling that I do not survive this. Every slight movement was a stabbing experience. I don't recall anymore what the food was like, but I know that I fell constantly asleep while eating. After my release from rehabilitation, Mr. Pollock worked with me. The day arrived to go for the deposition. The other party agreed to two half day depositions. I got quite nervous and concerned whether I would understand all the questions. On the second day of the depositions, the attorney from the other party tried to trick me into a question and Mr. Pollock spoke out, which was then recorded on the tape. When everything was all over, I won the case. I very much appreciated the wisdom and knowledge of Mr. Pollock. It was quite interesting to see how he handled my case. It was also a lot of work on my part. I needed to keep every single receipt from doctors and other treatments I had to endure. When the case was completed, Mr. Pollock handed all the papers over to me. I didn't put them on a scale. I couldn't carry them because of the weight.

Most parents of my Day Care children remained in contact with me, even when I moved and they were no longer my clients. This made me feel good that I was appreciated. I continued to see the children grow up through the pictures they sent me.

For a while, I had some part time help. Her name was Amy. We had already moved to our new home in Parker, where we had the master bedroom on the first floor. With our granddaughter in our care, she attended the preschool and Kindergarten at Prairie Crossing Elementary School, which was across the street from our house.

When our grandson was born in 2004, we didn't have custody of him yet. He also needed surgeries for his clubfoot. When the mother brought her son to us and left for the day, he was only a few months old, I sensed that the end of their marriage was near. My husband and I decided to apply for custody for him, too. This was an even more costly affair. It also was extremely stressful. Our attorney recommended involving a family psychologist, which we did. During this process, I also decided to adopt some birds. I drove to the Gabriel Foundation in Elizabeth and looked for adoptable birds for our situation. Our granddaughter wanted a cockatiel. So we took home two Nanday conures and a cockatiel. These two Nandays loved to sit on my shoulders at all times, but this was impossible. I had purchased a large cage for the dining room. When we had dinner, they screeched and would fly to me. Their names were Oscar and Jill. Jill always said thank you when he received an almond or a peanut. I loved these two parrots, but they were extremely loud, and they wanted to sit all day long on my shoulders. This I couldn't tolerate. I was afraid when I was cooking that they would get hurt or poop. My family told me that I have to return them. This was difficult for me, but I understood them. I learned afterwards that they found another good home.

We stopped by at the Dumb Friends League in Denver. I then fell in love with two lutino lovebirds. They stayed together in one cage and needed to be adopted together. We took them home. At the time of my writing this, it happened ten years ago. One is still alive and quite active. When his friend was close to death and could no longer go to the drinking bowl, Kirby would fill his beak with water and went over to Lacey. Lacey opened his beak and Kirby put the water in. This touched me so deeply how creatures care for one another. Kirby screamed when Lacey died. I took Lacey out, wrapped him in towels, and my husband buried him in the roses in our backyard. Next to Kirby's cage stood another cage with four budgies. Kirby sat on the side and looked over. It seemed to me that he wanted to join them. However lovebirds can attack the big Macaws because they think they are the biggest and the strongest. I then asked the expert of the Gabriel Foundation about my situation and Kirby. I was advised to place Kirby to the budgies because he might want to be part of their flock, but I must watch him closely. I then transferred Kirby to the budgies. Kirby seemed to be jealous of the budgies' longer tails and constantly tried to pick on one of them. Every time Kirby went after one of the budgie's tail, I squirted him with water. I stayed with them in the sunroom all day long. It worked out.

2004   Indonesian tsunami
Madrid train bombings
Beslan school hostage crisis in Russia
George W. Bush reelected president

In 2004, we drove with Irene and Peter to Dresden in the former East Germany, then on to Prague, the capital and largest city of the Czech Republic or Czechoslovakia. On the way to our destination, we saw a large Star of David. I wanted to see the reason behind it. It was so huge, and I said to Irene and Peter, "Let's stop! I like to know what this building is all about!" I knew we were in Terezin, but I didn't know its meaning. We soon found out that this is also called Theresienstadt. Then we knew that this was a former concentration camp of the SS or Nazis. We stopped and visited the museum. Terezin was originally a walled city and small fortress in Czechoslovakia built in the 1800's to protect the river and roads in the area. When Nazi Germany took over much of Czechoslovakia in 1939, they renamed the town of 7000 Theresienstadt. Plans began to convert the town and fortress into a concentration camp for Jews and "non-Aryans". What we saw is indescribable. My personal experience was when we entered that place that everything must have happened just recently. We went through all the rooms, even it is now a museum. You still feel the ground crying to heaven. Over ten years have passed since we visited this museum, but I still feel the anguish what happened in reality, which was by far more cruel and painful. I almost felt ashamed that I was a German once, but on the other hand, I was not even born or just an infant when all this happened. Also, the majority of the Germans didn't know about it. My parents were not filled with hate toward the Jewish people. Heppenheim had once a synagogue and quite a few Jewish citizens. I own a book about the Jews from Heppenheim. Their names are listed and the date when they got picked up and what happened to them, but initially, they sold to the locals the words *work camps*. Terezin was not a death camp like Dachau, but killings and starvation took place, too. From Terezin we continued on to Prague.

On the way, we stopped at the place of St. Elizabeth of Hungary, T.O.S.F., also known as Saint Elizabeth of Thuringia, a princess of the Kingdom of Hungary, Landgravine of Thuringia, Germany. She is a greatly venerated Catholic saint. Elizabeth was married at the age of fourteen and widowed at 20. After his death, she sent her children away and regained her dowry, using the money to build a hospital where she herself served the sick. She became a symbol of Christian charity after her death at age 24 and was quickly canonized.

Our next stop was Wittenberg, the place of Martin Luther and the 95 Theses. This little town in eastern Germany doesn't look like the center of a revolution. But the events that played out there in the 16th century shook the foundation of Christendom.

My husband was the driver, and when we arrived in Praque, he immediately received a ticket. The police was standing right there and waited already for the next victim. It was a tricky spot in the downtown area. What a wonderful welcome this was for us. The Vitava or Moldau is the longest river in the Czech Republic and beautifies the city of Prague, the capital of the Czech Republic. It is also called "the City of a Hundred Spires" and is also known for its Old Town Square, the heart of its historic core, with colorful baroque buildings, Gothic churches and the medieval Astronomical Clock, which gives an animated hourly show. Prague has many points of interest and something for every taste. Some dishes are quite close to German recipes. The "steak tartare" is well known in Germany, too. It was one of my favorites, weather in Germany or the Czech Republic. It is raw beef that is cut and minced and is served with condiments and an egg on top. They also have the Wiener and Frankfurter sausages, but mainly served as fast food. Duck can also be found on many menus.

The experience in Terezin moved me so deeply that I had to write following poem when we arrived back home in the States.

A World filled with hate and greed
Why is the world filled with hate and greed
Why is there suffering and pain
Man has not sought an exalted desire
Yet Christ's death was not in vain

His love is immense and continues on
He obeyed his Father's will
That all could experience heaven's bliss
The cross paid us sinners' bill

What can we learn from such noble love
This command was addressed to me
Search your heart was a sudden response
Seek Me out and soon you will see

Gazing at Him from the depth of my soul
Was a meet I could not imagine
The voiceless message that was given to me
Was by far not of human origin

What was shown to me was love divine
A love that is difficult to grasp
Yet turning heavenwards, asking for help
Will heal me and will also heal you
        -Rita Lulay Malsch, OCDS

2005   Hurricane Katrina
        Pope John Paul II dies
        London terrorist bombings
2006   Saddam Hussein is convicted and hanged in
        Baghdad
        Pluto is reclassified a dwarf planet

In 2006, my brother-in-law, Alfons, celebrated his 70th birthday. Marianne, with her acting talent, made already plans for a fun evening. We didn't want to miss this and booked three flights to Germany. What I didn't know was that I was a target for a major part in a play. When Marianne informed me what I needed to do and say, I replied, "I cannot do that!" However, I didn't want to be a party-pooper and accepted the assignment. She handed me a sheet with instructions and told me to study it. Two days later we had our first practice, a second one the following day, and two days later was Alfons' birthday and the performance. Everything took place at the Villa Rosemary in Kirschhausen. It was a successful evening. All the pictures proof it.

We four sisters act out a play for the 70ᵗʰ birthday of my brother-in-law, Alfons

My husband was away in Montana. I decided to clean the bird cage with undiluted bleach. Lacey the lovebird bit me that it bled. I then cleaned the big cage with the bleach. I don't know what happened, but when my son came home, he found me on the floor unconscious. I was then admitted to the hospital. They kept me overnight for observation. I was discharged the next day. It could have been a seizure, or the fumes from the bleach and the wound from Lacey's bite, or just the extreme stress we had to endure with the custody situation.

When I felt fine again, I decided for another bird, for an African Grey parrot. I got in contact with a breeder in Arizona. She had babies, but they were still too young to go to a home. I had to wait a few weeks. We all looked forward to this parrot when we drove to the Denver International Airport to pick up Nikki, the name I had planned on giving the parrot. After her first night at our house, I had scheduled an appointment with an avian veterinarian. He checked the bird for its sex, so I learned that the bird was female. He had also asked me whether I wanted to have the wings clipped. I said NO. She should have the freedom to fly around. When we returned home, Nikki flew high up to the window sill, at least nine feet, and we couldn't get her down. We were hoping that she would fly down on her own, but not so. We had to place a tall ladder on the wall to get her. Without a problem, she decided to fly down on her own. I'm sure she was hungry, too. I called immediately for another appointment with the veterinarian to get the wings clipped. She was recently ten years old and is a wonderful feathered companion. She calls our names and really participates with what is going on in the house. At times she can be hilarious. In the morning, when our grandson was still in Kindergarten, she would call his name and say in a demanding voice, "Get dressed!" or to this day, if something falls on our hardwood floor and makes a loud noise, she asks, "What happened?" She asks me quite often, "What are you doing?" When I give her breakfast, I cook for my parrots the MASH diet, she won't start feeding herself until I take her beak between my thumb and my pointed finger and move it from side to side and greet her, "Good morning, Nikki! You want your breakfast?"

The custody ordeal for our grandson was finally over and we didn't need to go to court. I wouldn't want to go through this again. The entire situation spoke for us. The raising of two small children, our grandchildren, was not always easy as long as the other party lived in town. When she moved out of state, working with the children became easier because she had less influence on them. Dealing with doctors and teachers had become part of my life, too. Our granddaughter had severe eczema and asthma. She was hospitalized several times. Our grandson has ADHD. Life is never boring. Our granddaughter struggled very much in her first year in High School. She called quite often from school and said that she is sick and needs to be picked up. She is doing fine now. Our grandson is still in Middle School, but I hope and pray that his ADHD will not interfere too much with his studies.

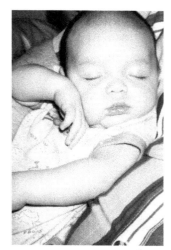

Our granddaughter (two years old), our grandson (infant)

I took an online course in Birdie Basics. After completion, I contacted Professor S.G. Friedman, Ph.D., and signed up for the intensive parrot behavior seminar. At the beginning of 2008, I completed this highly interesting online seminar ***Living and Learning with Parrots; the Fundamentals of Behavior.***

2008 Cuban president Fidel Castro permanently steps down after 49 years in power
Barack Obama elected U.S. president

Klaus Peter and I

In March of 2008 was my last trip to Germany. Klaus Peter and I took our two grandchildren along. We had rented an apartment in Kirschhausen during our visit. We made day trips, visited the Starkenburg Castle, saw my sisters, nieces and nephews, and we hosted a party at the Schaefer restaurant. The restaurant is quite famous for its delicious menus, and the owner is a nephew of my deceased brother-in-law, Fridolin. I had to make reservations in advance from the United States. It was a successful afternoon with good food and sharing many stories. Two nieces, who are also sisters, surprised us with their belly dancing talents and their colorful belly dance costumes. The following week we drove to Hohenstein and visited Klaus Peter's cousin, Wolfgang with his spouse. We dined at the Hohenstein Castle, which was quite exciting for our grandchildren. During the 30-year War, the castle was destroyed and never re-built. The ruin is in good condition, but restoration is planned. It is also being used as a backdrop for plays.

Being connected with the Carmelite Mission in Tanzania, East Africa, I wrote the following poem:

The Missionary
I admire the man or woman
Who goes to a foreign land
To help the poor and forgotten
With his or her gentle hands

He listens to God's calling
To leave home and family
For the sake of all God's children
To guide all to sanctity

He cares for the sick and dying
Teaches the deaf and blind
He also trains the handicapped
With his God given mind

He brings the message of the Lord
To those who walk in darkness
He lives the love of Jesus
With much patience and kindness

A missionary doesn't fear
The mountain's bitter cold
Or the burning heat of Africa
He is always strong and bold

He is a man or woman of prayer
This sustains him to go on
Without this noble dialogue
Everything would go wrong

Of persecution he is not afraid
This very often is present
Or painful hunger or martyrdom
Yet he knows why he was sent

He walks this earth like the Son of Man
Nowhere to lay his head
Freely he gives his entire self
Ensures that all are fed

To serve the family of God
Has made him a person of vision
His dedication is not a sport
His life is one big mission

Let's share God's goodness we have received
With all those who are in need
That we too can rejoice and Christ will say
We have become brothers and sisters indeed
                    --Rita Lulay Malsch, OCDS

2009 US Airways Flight 1549 emergency landing in Hudson River
2010 Massive 7.0 earthquake hits Haiti
          Explosion on BP oil rig causes largest marine oil spill in history

During the summer break, Klaus Peter booked four flights to San Diego, California. He used our accumulated mileage. Our son chose to take the train. We visited the *Sea World*. The children were so fascinated by the orcas and their performances, and our granddaughter was chosen to assist with tricks acted out by the sea lions. It was a wonderful experience for all of us to see what these creatures are able to do. We continued on to the Zoo. The San Diego Zoo is a zoo in Balboa Park, San Diego, California. It houses over 3,700 animals of more than 650 species. You could spend days or even weeks at the zoo in order to see all the animals. The time was over quickly and we needed to fly back to Denver, Colorado.

One day, I received a message from my sister, Agnes, that Irene was very ill and has breast cancer. She informed me that shortly before the diagnosis, Irene would eat only small amounts of food. Every Sunday, Irene and Peter drove to Heppenheim to meet with Agnes and Alfons. When Peter, her husband, announced in the early evening to go back home to Abtsteinach, Irene always wanted to stay longer with Agnes and Alfons. I was always concerned about their marriage. In a very short time, Irene got very ill and was only able to eat baby food. Her son, Richard and his wife, Nicole, arranged with me to talk to Irene via Skype. When I saw her, I was shocked and searched for words to say something to her. Then I asked her whether she could eat. She nodded. It was probably not the best question. She was very weak and didn't say anything. Nicole and Richard brought her back to the bed. She then waved at me. I realized that Irene had recognized me, but that I would not see her again. She wore a flamingo night gown contrasting her black hair. She looked very pretty. Her facial expression had changed. She died a few days later in the hospital in Heppenheim on July 23, 2010. She wanted so badly to visit us again, but cancer didn't allow it and triumphed.

In 2010, we adopted our dog, Lacy, when she was two years old. She is a Terrier/Chihuahua mix and quite lovable and intelligent. When she needs to go outdoors for her duty, she stands in front of you and stares into your eyes. When you ask her, "Do you have to go out?" She goes around in circles and is happy that you asked this question and runs to the door. At night, she licks your hand, if she needs to go, but it doesn't happen often.

2011   Japan 9.0 magnitude earthquake and tsunami lead to nuclear accident
Obama bin Laden killed
Arab Spring

Seven months after my sister's death, I had my third spine surgery on February 14, 2011. It was also Valentine's Day. I was in so much pain that I could no longer postpone it and needed to get things fixed. My husband drove me to SkyRidge Medical Center in Lone Tree, Colorado. When I woke up after the surgery, but was still half asleep from the anesthesia, my surgeon came in and visited me. Shortly before, I had noticed that I couldn't move my legs. However, I was still sleepy and it didn't register. I asked the doctor, "Am I paralyzed?" He answered me, "I'm so sorry." Then I knew it. After the surgery, my surgeon and the anesthesiologist informed my husband that they had lost contact with my legs. They had opened me up again, checked everything, and that I had to undergo an MRI. However, they couldn't find anything wrong. They said to my husband that it could have been a spinal stroke, even so they didn't know for sure. I stayed in the hospital for ten days. My surgeon had arranged for me to be moved to Craig Hospital for rehabilitation. I needed to be approved by Craig Hospital. A lady came to visit me and had many questions. They accepted me. This was not what I had anticipated when I went for surgery. At Craig Hospital, I had my own television in the room, but the nurse woke me up and moved me to the other side every two hours in order not to get open bed sores. I hated that and wanted to sleep at night. After two weeks I was transferred to another room. It had an extra bed for my husband, a spacious kitchen with refrigerator, a large couch with table for guests, and a huge window. It was nice, but I told my treating physician every day, "I want to walk and I want to go home!" This was easier said than done. As most of the patients there have spinal cord or brain injuries, you needed some assistance to adjust to this tragic situation. I met every other day with a psychologist at Craig Hospital. Then the work started. I had a hard time finding my way around. Craig Hospital is so huge. The days were filled with various treatments and the FES bike. Riding an FES bike simulates the physical activity that a person normally experiences during an average day. Cycling for one hour is equivalent to walking 6,000 steps. My surgeon visited me almost every

ISABELL VON DER WALDESRUH

Saturday, and my sisters Agnes and Marianne skyped with me every Sunday. Edith and some other friends surprised me once in a while. Mary Frances and Pat and some other people brought me Holy Communion. I was hardly to be found in my room. JoAnn from the Parker Artist Guild left me some flowers, probably from her garden. Father Marlon, OCD, tried to visit me, but we saw each other only once. The ten weeks I lived there seemed like eternity, no end in sight.

Three days before my discharge, another therapist worked with me and probably didn't get the right instructions. We stood at the window in my room and she said to me, "Stand!" I tried to stand, but collapsed because I couldn't stand. In the afternoon, Lucy from the Carmelite Community visited me and I told her that I fell earlier. I had no pain or anything, but in the middle of the night, I had so much pain that the nurse had to call my doctor from Craig Hospital. They gave me some kind of medication. The next day, I couldn't feed myself because when I lifted my arms, they would fall right down. I couldn't even call my husband. I was upset because everyone ignored me completely after this incident. My discharge day was in less than a week. I told my physician that I cannot go home under these conditions. I was so scared. I was then told that the medications I got after the fall didn't agree with my other medications. One of the nurses yelled at me and said, "Don't make me call the doctor in the middle of the night again!" I had the feeling that they were afraid I would sue them. My physician had ordered X-rays. When he had received the results, he told me to see an orthopedic doctor when I get home. I felt hurt by this kind of treatment. My cousin in Austin, Texas, called me almost every night. I will never forget that. She helped me so much, and I was able to share with her the hurt I experienced. I was discharged as planned but did not return for my six months check up. I was still very troubled by this treatment before my discharge.

When I arrived at my home, it felt like I had been away for a very long time. There was now a ramp in front of the house. I realized that something deep inside me had changed since I had left close to three months ago. My being was severed. This included my soul, body, and spirit. I wasn't sure whether I was happy or close to tears. Now I needed to adjust to my own home and to my handicapped condition. The question came to me will I depend on people for the rest of my life. At Craig Hospital, they couldn't tell me whether I would walk again. My husband had sold my car, and my surgeon called me at home right after my discharge from Craig Hospital. The slightest improvement like a toe moving made him hopeful. Physical therapy, twice a week, started immediately. I had a good therapist. After several months of physical therapy, he had asked me to take a step. I didn't think that I would be able to. Before I could say anything else, he said, "Rita, you did your first step!" I said, "I did?" Every visit he placed me on the leg press. The left leg got stronger and stronger. The right leg increased in strength very slowly, but never got that far as the left one. Doing bed exercises for 30 minutes or longer every day can get frustrating and boring, but it is of great importance. I got the message that in order to exercise daily, I need to listen to music. The music I already owned was okay, but I needed something new, something different. I ran across the famous German tenor *Fritz Wunderlich.* He sang the Italian folk song *Tiritomba,* which I sang as a teenager. I ordered a CD which included that song. Listening to him transported me into another world. I realized that his songs, his voice, are in harmony with me. I ordered the *Vogelhaendler* and more. I also own a Christmas CD from him. The song *Was soll das bedeuten es taget ja schon* goes back to the year 1656 A.D. by Daniel Paur, Innsbruck, Austria. I sang this also as a child and have never heard it again in modern times. Unfortunately, Fritz Wunderlich died in 1966 at the age of 35. He fell down the stairs and died the next day at the University Clinic of Heidelberg. He was a few weeks away from his Metropolitan Opera debut in New York City as Tamino in Mozart's *The Magic Flute.* He is buried in Munich's Waldfriedhof cemetery. My other favorite group are the *Kastelruther Spatzen.* This is a musical group from South Tyrol, northern Italy. Their songs are in the German language. They dedicated one song on one of their CDs especially to Pope Benedict XVI. The Holy Father in return expressed through their manager his benediction.

2012 London Olympics
Hurricane Sandy
Barack Obama reelected
2013 Pope Benedict XVI resigns
Pope Francis elected
Nelson Mandela dies
2014 Sochi Olympics
Russian Federation annexes Crimea
IFA World Cup in Brazil
Ebola crisis deepens
ISIS

In 2013, my neurologist retired and I had to find a new one. I approached my primary care physician and he referred me to one. He said to me to find a good neurologist is difficult. The neurologist he referred me to was not well liked. He didn't go into detail. Then I made an appointment with this new neurologist. I found him pleasant. After a while, he said we should change your seizure medication to a newer one. Well, I was all for it, even I had no absence seizures and felt okay. I started this newer medication, and after a while, I sensed that my condition was going the wrong direction. He prescribed an additional medication. I just didn't feel happy the way things were going. I complained to him. He told me you have anxiety. I wondered why would I have anxiety all of a sudden. This went on for almost an entire year. I was not happy at all and didn't know what to do. In the morning of Christmas Eve 2014, I had an appointment with him. At that time he told me that he wants to discontinue all medication. I said NO and left it with that. I just stared at him in distrust. I was upset. In the afternoon, I had one major seizure after another, which I never had in my entire life. My husband called the neurologist. He instructed my husband to call the ambulance. At the hospital, I was in critical condition for an hour because atrial fibrillation had started on top of it, most likely from the seizures. They kept me over Christmas in the ICU. When I was discharged, I saw this neurologist one more time. He just told my husband and me, "If this happens again, to call him right away." I didn't want this to happen a second time. During my hospital stay, the neurologist from the hospital increased the seizure medication, but it didn't change anything. I had to find another neurologist. This time I was doing it on my own. I asked for my records from the neurologist and from the hospital. The ones from the neurologist were totally screwed up that I reported him to the Medical Board of Colorado. I read in my hospital records that the neurologist reported that I saw him in the morning for severe backache and that the pain was getting worse. This was completely false. I had no backache since my spine surgery in 2011. There were two other things that were incorrect. I added an addendum to my hospital records. How things turned out for the neurologist with the Medical Board, I do not know. It remains a secret. I was offered to go for rehabilitation after the hospital stay. However, I declined because I wanted to go home. The hospital physician ordered physical therapy at my house. Carol, a wonderful and knowledgeable lady, worked with me three times a week. When the insurance no longer would cover her visits, I asked her if she could still see me on a private basis, which she accepted. With her assistance, I learned to walk stairs. She liked my paintings and purchased some. It was no longer a patient and therapist relationship. We had also become good friends. She had answers to all my questions.

I found a neurologist who specializes in seizures. I had left the one who would not listen to my many concerns with his prescribed medication. My new neurologist placed me on a walking EEG for a few days. After studying it, she decided that I should go back to my previous medication that kept me seizure free.

Over two years have passed since this episode, and I remain seizure free. I continue to exercise daily in bed for half-an-hour to remain strong in my legs. Because I can do basically everything while sitting down in the wheelchair, but a timer will remind me every 45 minutes to walk around with the walker. I need to do this in order to keep my present condition and my legs strong. It helps also to control my weight. This is very difficult to do. I'm happy to say that I just started the Mayo Clinic Diet and I'm still following their proven philosophy.

I do not get out of the house often because I no longer drive, so I decided at the end of 2016 to adopt more feathered friends - two more budgies, two masked lovebirds, and two Senegal parrots. I cook for them the MASH diet. This recipe calls for fifteen different beans, fruits, vegetables, and grains. They love it, especially when they are hungry. It took a short time for them to adjust to the new food. The color is not appealing at all. It is an ugly green. I add ground walnuts, fresh parsley daily to the MASH and Cayenne pepper. Now they fight when they see their breakfast. Especially the budgies become quite ill-tempered at one another and pick on each other.

2015 Lithuania establishes the euro as its official currency

Massacres continue in Nigeria by the Boko Haram group

2016 Donald J. Trump elected president

Cooking was always something I enjoyed. Initially, I was afraid when I still lived at my mother's house before I got married. Now when something needs to be served quickly, I follow my inner guide. I cut potatoes in half inch pieces and steam them. In no time, I'm able to brown an onion in a pan with canola oil, add the potatoes, minced garlic, Italian seasoning, celery salt, ham or sausage pieces, and green onions. I top the dish with fresh parsley. This is always a welcomed meal and is done relatively fast.

Years back, I loved to collect stamps and purchased rare ones. After a while I lost interest. I then designed two large canvas boards with German stamps and had them framed.

I still draw and paint. I donated ten 36" x 36" paintings to the Salvation Army. Now I use canvas boards, drawing paper, and watercolor paper. Framed paintings are more appealing to me and to potential customers than stretched canvas paintings. My paintings made it twice to the International Peace Exhibition at the International Peace Museum in Nagasaki, Japan.

I was juried into many shows, and I'm currently in another juried show *Imagine: Fairy Tales & Beyond* at Deep Space at the Art District in Parker, Colorado. I chose the Fairy Tales *Red Riding Hood, Frog Prince,* and *Rumpelstiltskin.* I belong to the Parker Artist Guild. We have a few venues in Parker and the Arapahoe Justice Center where members of the PAG can show and sell their art works. It is always a good feeling when I sell a piece or get accepted into a juried show. I also drew a self-portrait with Prismacolor colored pencils and I'm pleased how it turned out.

I started journaling many years ago but would pause for a while and then continue on again. There was also a time when I loved to write poetry and haiku. The desire to write poetry is not always present. I also love to translate English to German and the other way around. For a while I translated articles from English to German for a religious organization in Texas.

I know a lot of people from around the world. Family members live in Johannesburg and Cape Town, South Africa. In Queensland, Australia, reside more cousins with their families, including the United Kingdom and Germany.

I belong to the Art Colony which is a fun, friendly on-line community for visual artists working in painting, drawing, mixed media, sculpture, and handicrafts. These artists are from all over the world, whether it is Malaysia or South America. It is also fun to see other cultures through their art. I also post my art on *Fine Art America, Artstack, Twitter,* and *Facebook.*

Reading my life's ups and downs with its various experiences and happenings, I have many questions for myself and God.

What would have happened if my father would not have died at such a young age? I most likely would have flourished like any other child. The choice to attend a school for higher learning would have been a high priority. I strongly believe that the University of Heidelberg would have been my first choice to study medicine and then use these skills as a missionary among the forgotten on this earth. Was the seizure disorder triggered by my father's death or not? If I would have remained in Germany and never placed a foot on American soil, what other path would have been an option? I contemplate many more open questions. They are all justified. I could pursue each question and write more stories. They all would be good, but I wrote my story as it happened in real time, a road less traveled.

I can ask my Creator why he chose this road for me. He probably would answer me, "You chose this journey under my guidance." So I'm happy with my life with all its mountains and valleys. Even my handicap has many great blessings. I can no longer drive a car, but I can paint and draw, write letters, poems, and prayers. I also love to cook healthy meals for my family and on and off invite someone to cultivate friendships. I still have health issues. The daily pain and burning in my legs, which most likely will remain until I leave this earth, are companions that remind me that this life is not forever. I trust that something much better awaits me. This gives me great joy.

Looking back
Looking back at my life
From where I stand now
I see the Lord's footprints
Beside me in a row

When I was younger
I didn't hear him talk
Nor did I feel his closeness
Alone did I walk

When I began blossoming
As the years moved on
I searched and found him
I named him MY SONG

He had become my music
He asked me for a dance
I could not refuse him
And gave it a chance

Affection overwhelmed me
When he stroked my hair
His spirit had touched me
With a celestial flair

What a sublime experience
To be one with my Lord
I will never leave him
I don't fear the sword
           --Rita Lulay Malsch, OCDS

CPSIA information can be obtained
at www.ICGtesting.com
Printed in the USA
FFHW011256050119
50064179-54881FF